Truework, are you?

Workplace observations and elements of NLP Coaching

Anna Kelly

I0462005

PublishNation
www.publishnation.co.uk

Dedicated to my parents

Elizabeth and Richard Kelly

And those whom I am close to, they know who they are

CONTENTS

FOREWORD

I work with clients to "Take Concrete" Steps to achieve career goals, the Coaching Program must be designed to meet the requirements and needs of each customer. The program is structured in a way that ensures the confidence to find the right career, encouragement and inspiration. It reduces fear, vulnerability and anxiety, the factors that help people to decide their future.

I was baffled by the expert advice given to students, handed out like candies in brightly covered packaging. Suddenly, various charities and organizations claim to be specialists in this area of knowledge. I am A career Coach and I really like going to schools to conduct dummy interviews, knowledge and excellent quality Advice on employment/careers for the present and for the future.

There is much more to career coaching than meets the eye, at the beginning it is about the person getting to know themselves, believe me, it is not as easy as it seems. These "experts" tell students to go online to complete personality tests to learn about themselves. This notion could help to small degree, but the underlying skills and talents are not shine through. So, these tests in practice are useless, a taste of the "fun" personality tests featured in glossy magazines.

Many companies are now organizing community assistance programs and releasing staff to attend these sessions as interviewers. Undoubtedly some will be really interested in the plan for the good reasons. Others will see it as an opportunity to pursue their own career and for others it will be a day away from work.

My concern is that these sessions will provide a variety of knowledge elements based on the interviewer. I firmly believe and know Career Coaches provide a better insight into the work environment and how to achieve true success.

I can open the door to any business without getting into the reception area which is just one of the skills I can offer. I have seen examples of online CVS offered by these "experts" and, unfortunately, the standards fall very short to ensure employability.

To be honest, if I needed construction work done, I would go to a construction contractor not the greengrocer and of course, vice versa. So why, schools do not use the skills and knowledge that are provided by career coaches.

The government has still claim that students are lacking in basic interview techniques, the stories I'm told by companies is amazing. The students who turn up for interviews with bad attitudes, unprepared and disinterested at all levels.

My advice to everyone is to get a good career coaching for now and the future.

Regards

Anna

What Has Some Large Companies and Cyber bullying Got in Common?

Hi Everyone,

Great to see the sun and a clear blue sky, nature is a wonderful thing as it soothes us, and we can realise the calmer, gentler side of life.

This week, so far, I have been appalled, disgusted, you name it at the cavalier attitude of some employers, an understatement really. What examinations, if any, what texts have been read by them because many of them have clearly discarded any formal training they received.

We are reading in the press constantly of cyber bullying, I hope my presentations in schools will help to elevate this problem. Society has broken down, in business there are areas that have broken down due to a range of factors, lack of sufficient training, lack of business intelligence, lack of knowledge and lack of principles making way for "1 don't care less" attitude. I am sure if I asked many managers what the management principles were, they would not know the answer.

Sad, that Merrill Lynch must operate a "Magic Roundabout" system for their staff, a method whereby staff work through the night, a taxi takes an employee home at 7am, waits for him/her to shower and change and then promptly takes them back to work to continue with the day shift! We are back to the days of The Industrial Revolution and many of us do not recognise the fact.

I attended the Chamber Group Expo 2013, which was an interesting, useful event and as always enjoyable. But I was perturbed by a story I heard; money was stolen from a safe, two employees had access, neither would admit the crime. The employer dismissed both. Bad move, it would have been better to have involved the police, who are trained to investigate. Such action has the potential to damage the management and company/s reputation, and the innocent party if there was one.

Or maybe a company's reputation does not matter these days, I can certainly name one company who is not interested in staff welfare. Maybe they are too big, and government backed so appear untouchable. It has been brought to my attention that this large organisation fails to understand what the word investigate means. And unfortunately, believe that they can "skirt" around issues, failing therefore to resolve human issues. They are convinced that "Human Resources" does not relate to human beings. So out the window goes self-respect, loyalty to the business and common decency for our fellow human beings.

I hope that I can encourage these "human "resource managers to attend my seminar. I believe that they need to return to basics of personnel management. The days when people in this field of work were trained to resolve business relationships with success. Currently, there is an on-going case whereby the frustrated employee has made 61 requests to the "Human" Resources to view evidence in support of bullying and intimidation. Such refusals can only lead to speculation that all is not as it should be in such an organisation. Sending our signals that there is a bullying management culture and therefore such behaviour goes unchecked. And of course, will continue for evermore, until a person with personnel knowledge, self —respect and very sound management skills arrives like a breath of fresh air to the company.

There are companies who are crazy with power and arrogance. They consider their staff like a knife and fork, needed for the job, after that they are not important or required. Managers who think that to make a profit; their staff must be treated less than fair. If it were possible it could be a breach of the Trade Descriptions Act. My professional advice to "Human "Resource managers is, ask yourself three questions. Firstly, why did you want to be a human resource person? Are you complying with what the job description suggests? Should the word "human" be omitted from your job titles and description?

I think at times, when I hear such horrible stories of ill-treatment at the hands of unscrupulous managers. The Government should consider introducing a new act of parliament to make it a criminal act for mistreatment in the workplace. What a deterrent that would be!!

Credit to the CEO of the call centre, in the programme of the same name on BBCI on Wednesday nights. That CEO certainly cares for his staff. Watch closely, there are some lessons to be learnt in dealing with lateness and bad timekeeping.

Bye for now, until next time

Anna

The core concepts within NLP and in relation to career coaching.

NLP, the term being Neuro, the human mind and body. Linguistic, the language. Programming, the mapping of construct: Thus, meaning all our senses, sight, sound, touch, taste and smell interact to impact on thought processes influencing behaviour towards how situations and circumstances are viewed. This technique has been used for years as a behaviour changing process from maladaptive to positive thought patterns. Used widely in the fields of hypnotherapy and psychotherapy to overcome negative beliefs, the concept being reframing. Dependent upon the client, the NLP elements can be used solely or incorporated into the client's programme.

Founded in the 1970's by Richard Bandler and John Grinder under the tutelage of noted anthropologist Gregory Bateson at California University, who was influenced by Alfred Korzybski at Esalen Institute. Particularly his ideas about human modelling that the map "is not the territory'.

The co-founders of NLP were interested in the exceptional skills of therapists Fritz Perts, Virginia Satir, Milton H Erickson and subsequently two books were published. Bandler and Grinder worked with and separately in the late 1970's with Leslie Cameron-Bandler, Judith DeLozier, Robert Dilts and David Gordon to contribute to the development of NLP.

Unfortunately, in the 1980's Bandler and Grinder fell out resulting in lawsuits, NLP began to be developed haphazardly by differing individuals. Following this, a successful UK practitioner evoked the trademark "NLP" as a generic term rather than intellectual property. Finally, in 2001 it was legally settled that Bandler and Grinder were to be known as the co-founders of NLP.

John Grinder worked with other people to develop the New Code of NLP, a mind, body systemic approach. Richard Bandier introduced new processes based on sub modalities and Ericksonian hypnosis. Is NLP a science? There have been many opinions regarding the true formulation of NLP and training programmes are in practice, Australia has the only official authority.

Psycholinguist William Levelt stated, "NLP is not informed about linguistics literature, it is based on vague insights that were out of date, their linguistics concepts are not properly construed or are mere fabrications, and conclusions are based upon the wrong premises". William concluded that NLP had nothing to do with neuroscientific insights, linguistics, informatics or theories of programming. Michael Corballis agreed with William's statements saying, "NLP is a thoroughly fake title, designed to give the impression of scientific respectability". An opposing opinion was made by Jaap Hollander, encouraging a better relationship with NLP processes and science. Jaap stated "qualitative scientific inquiry bears a striking resemblance with the process of modelling in NLP".Robert Dilts and Judith DE Lozier clearly conveyed the difference by stating that it was important to recognise that NLP was more subjective and systematically oriented than objective and deterministic sciences. As a science NLP was more qualitative than quantitative, more structuralist than materialistic.

NLP assumes that the senses are limited, if so, then a person perceives only a small part of "the world" through the process. The core elements are rapport in communication; NLP highlights indirect communication of the senses to bring about positive change e.g. "I see a bright future ahead". Communication is a very powerful tool and should be used to full effect to obtain a good client assessment and outcome. NLP has three core concepts, Modelling/Mapping, Reframing and Anchoring.

Modelling or Mapping, like qualitative research uses data from naturalistic settings and inductive analysis of the data. Basically, the client mirrors the behaviours and core beliefs of a person who has achieved excellence in their field of work. Because external factors in the subconscious can influence perceptions, the mind acts as a filtration system, information can be lost, and views can be generalized, or hidden areas come to the fore. This is shown by body language, basically by overt and covert behaviour. However, if Modelling is successful, the client achieves self-fulfilment. Behaviour changes to those of the "model". The "Model" can be constructed to suit the client's hierarchy framework clearly showing goals or ambitions, using the client assessment. The hierarchy framework based on Maslow' is drawn as a pyramid, beginning with "self", moving up the pyramid, covering goals and aims at w relationships, and social status finally reaching the top to the fulfilment of "self".

Anchoring; whereby associations are made between sensations and emotional states "This status can be both empowering and disempowering depending on past experiences or environmental setting, either positive or negative. Assess the anchors as desired or purposive to support the client in their fulfilment.

Reframing; this is changing the way an event is perceived and therefore changing the meaning of that event. By reframing the language, the consequential responses and behaviours will also change giving a better view of the client's world. Importantly any behaviour change must be compatible with the client's natural and social environments otherwise other problems can ensue.

The client wanting change identifies the role and the action to be taken, seeing things from an objective perspective. Then deciding what can be done to be less predictable, change where and how things are done ready to have an appropriate hidden agenda for success.

What Does Your Staff and Customers Mean to You? How Far Would You Go to Destroy Them?

Hi everyone,

It has been a while since my last blog, due to work commitments. Congratulations to Andy Murray for becoming Wimbledon Champion, it was great to witness an exciting event. The buzz of the crowd, the smell of strawberries and the flow of Pimm's. The game of ladies and gentlemen, the suffix of Miss or Mrs used without a blink of an eye by the umpire. The '"whites" worn by the players as protocol and the grace of a bygone age, when good manners were a sign of a good upbringing. I digress, this is a story of the opposite, and an assistant in a Sainsbury's supermarket struggled to serve a customer talking on her mobile phone. The customer could see no wrong and complained about the assistant! Back to tennis, the press made comparisons between Andy and the legendary Fred

Perry, their style of playing and ridiculously about their personal lives. Though I expect it makes for interesting reading and harmed no-one.

I have read many articles on advice on preparing school leavers for the workplace. On reading, sound advice has been given, but it lacks, the benefits of face to face coaching. Many questions can be answered; the unwritten knowledge can be shared with eager-eyed students, painting a picture of the world of employment in their minds. I hasten to add, that the cruel side of employment, the glaring headlines " a culture of all work and no play " in the UK is damaging family life, causing high stress levels and creating the inability to switch off from work is not shown to them.

It is rare that the good side of employment is highlighted, there is so much that is morally   wrong with business today. I know I have mentioned business ethics before in an article. Whistleblowing is to lose its bad stigma and to be a moral act to correct wrongs to safeguard the public and should be extended to safeguard staff too. But what happens when the business/organisation goes step by step into murky waters.

Professor (Baroness) Susan Greenfield believes that everyone in work should revel in their individuality and be happy and fulfilled. Everyone should have that right, unfortunately, not everyone does. The Royal Bank of Scotland has a reputation of a bullying management culture and allows its staff to face torture within the workplace and shows no compassion because power rules. Good luck to Ross McEwan, the newly appointed CEO to RBS. I sincerely hope he has the courage of a lion to clear RBS of the rotten wood within, no mean feat, but it can be done...get the right people for the job. By the way, when does Fred Goodwin's case go to court? It is shocking to read that RBS have set aside £385 million pounds to pay fines and lawsuits, it does not say much for the company's standards and the quality of training when employing staff.

Another shocking story, nurses are to be taught how to be compassionate, surely, that is a basic factor of becoming a nurse. Of course, there are lots of good nurses, but they do not get highlighted.

There is without a shadow of a doubt a lack of management and training skills that are vital to the growth of the economy. When you work and manage staff whether you like it or not there are moral ethics involved. So well done to The Archbishop of Canterbury, Justin Welby for speaking out against Wonga. It's is 'murder" not of the physical type towards customers to charge exorbitant rates of interest. A real case; (not Wonga) a man borrowed £500 in 1974, but the interest rates rose it to £60, OOO by 2000, makes you think?

It is also a "murder" not to treat your employees with respect and adhere to company policies when doing so.

"When you realise you've made a mistake take immediate steps to correct it and never deny your convictions just for the sake of peace and quiet.

Have a good week, the sun is beckoning to me and I am going to succumb.

Bye for now

Observing professional codes of ethics, even if they are not mandatory or prescribed by legislation:

Coaching is primarily about improving the life and performance of the client. Through a one to one relationship the coach is given access to the client's hopes and fears. As rapport is built and trust develops the coach also shares the client's aspirations and future goals. Because of this privileged position, with the aim to enrich the life of the client, but also a position unless care is exercised can cause harm.

The client chooses the focus of conversation; the coach listens and contributes observations and questions. Coaching accelerates the progress by providing greater focus and awareness of choices. The client is held responsible and accountable for their own progress to succeed.

Professional codes of ethics are in place to ensure that the client/coach relationship is conducted to the highest level of ethics, professionalism, integrity, honesty, transparency, care. accountability, confidentiality as permitted by the client or requested by law, mutual respect, therefore non-basis in attitudes e.g. Beliefs, cultural, religious or linguistic differences. Coaches should be aware of the impact their own beliefs and values and the effect these may have on their coaching. Coaching that reflects positively and responsibly on the coaching profession.

Professional ethics covers the understanding of the coaching agreement terms and conditions, costs, the process, the location and the frequency of sessions. The coach must guarantee that there is no conflict of interest.

Other core values are included, without them can result in the harm being done during the coaching processes, client care, from directing the client to recommending different coaches or resources that would be more appropriate to the client needs. Refraining from offering professional information and advice that is beyond competence. Or indeed false claims about the results of what the client will receive from the coaching process. Personal professional conduct, this is not abusing the client's trust to gain sexual, emotional, financial or any kind of professional advantage. The coach should not prolong a coaching relationship beyond the contract, only if the client no longer benefits from the coaching. The client can terminate the coaching relationship at any time during the process.

The coach must obtain the consent of the client before releasing information such as progress reports and other to the person who may be employing them. Coaches must inform clients of any personal situations or relationships which may have an adverse effect upon the coach/client relationship, agreement of appropriate action should be taken.

Coaches must maintain appropriate accurate records of their work with clients. Coaches should monitor the quality of their work and welcome feedback from clients and other professionals. This will benefit both the coach and client as the coach can continually monitor the quality and fitness to practice at a level that provides an effective service.

Is Solicitors Hiding behind the Internet in Attempt to deal with Cases?

Hi everyone,

The excitement of Wimbledon, the strawberries and cream, ice cool Pimm's and gorgeous sunshine. Some things never change the aura and good manners of Wimbledon tennis has never ceased.

It is a pity that the legal profession has lost its aura along the way, the once noble profession was passed from generation to generation. There was pride in having your father's or grandfather's name in clear crisp lettering over the entrance door.

Once inside the door, you knew you were in safe hands, you were going to be guided through the maze of legal jargon and documentation. All the evidence was going to be viewed at all angles, searching for points of law to strengthen your claim to whatever the problem was. A few visits were made to sit with your legal "friend" in pursuance of justice. Justice a strong and encouraging word which conjures up images of the good triumphing over bad filling you with confidence that legal knowledge, skills and wise intelligence was going to win the day.

it appears that life in the legal profession has got easier, everything is viewed as black and white, cases are marked with a percentage tag for the chance of winning, there is no place for the evidence that does not fall into a slot. So, doing a degree in Law appears to be an easy option for students, it is a lucrative business, is that the magnet or is it really the urge to see that justice is done always.

But we have come a long way from the personal professional touch of bygone days. Many solicitors conduct the client's affairs by phone or over the internet initially. Information vital to the case can be lost this way, how many people have been told by a solicitor to contact The Citizen's Advice Bureau to obtain advice on a legal matter or given the incorrect information over the phone!

Bring back the pride of being a solicitor, empathise with your clients to make the right decisions, think about what being in the legal profession really means to you, if it is all about money and an easy option then you are in the profession for the wrong reason.

"Choose a job you love, and you'll never have to work a day in your life. When faced with a challenging task act as though it's impossible to fail".

Until next week, Bye for now!

Regards, Anna

The important client assessment, part of the coaching programme

The client's requirements are paramount to the coaching process in establishing what the client expects. Continually practising a professional code of conduct, inclusive of mutual respect, no discrimination, no harassment nor conflict of interest. Legal compliance e.g. The Data Protection Act and client confidentiality are adhered to. The client has responsibility for their achievements, the coach has the responsibility to, direct, listen, observe, encourage, direct client self-discovery, the enthusiasm to help the client succeed, offering solutions, strategies and choices. Coaching concentrates on the clients' status and their enhancement of their careers. An honest assessment must be carried out by both parties. The coach must respect the rights and feelings of the client, who might have values, attitudes and opinions that differ from their own. There must be a clear agreement of what is to be achieved by the client and the level of coaching that will be provided, based on qualifications and experience of the coach. The coach must take reasonable steps to ensure that the client progresses, if the client does not progress then the coach must reduce the possible effects on the client. The Initial client assessment and in-depth discussions should include the client's life purpose questionnaire; establish key work skills and values, motivators and interests. After which, the client should be confident in their control of their workload. help in using time and resources, such as guidance from peer groups, mentors and technical help to the greatest advantage. Provide an understanding of priorities, time restraints, coping with career progression issues e.g. protection from political in-house fighting. After the assessment process the client should understand their personality type and what they have to offer in their career.

In the planning stage, using a template recording the progress the client is making, to be adjusted to suit the client's requirements and training goals. The template should be headed with the client's name. Then columns headed with the date, job plans and programmes and listing when the goals/tasks were achieved. Career plans and opportunities would have been discussed. Being aware of the organisation's evaluation of the client, the reasons for both success and failure have been analysed during the assessment.

At the end of the coaching programme, the complete process can be reviewed for achievements and advancement in the workplace, however small, and the question 'was it all worth it [1]', hopefully it will always be for the client and coach.

Coaches must be diligent in the understanding and implementing their clients' and their own legal obligations covered by; race, national origin, ethnicity, age, gender, sexual orientation, religion, language, disability, socioeconomic status, and unfair discriminatory practices.

Finally, clients must be made aware of the International Institute of Coaching statement of standards and ethics. All promotional materials, verbal and written must be legal and truthful. And for the coach's professional security, it is recommended that Indemnity Insurance be in place.

By abiding by Ethics and standards, is beneficial to the coach's abilities and profession and equally beneficial to the client. The client is not left feeling frustrated, let-down, intelligence undermined or disheartened as to no longer want to achieve success.

Life's Fulfilment

To achieve fulfilment in our lives is, where we want to be, who we want to be with, family and friends or place, to be satisfied. In our working life, we want to achieve something; to me it is achieving satisfaction in what I do, big or small — in fact not to waste life. We only have one life and that is very precious, and no-one has the right to wrath someone's aspirations and dreams.

My life purpose is to be happy, content and comfortable. To exercise control in choice of goals and not be, influenced by people who want to dampen my dreams, so I wrote a book, organised a dance to raise funds. Unfortunately, there are times when factors can hinder people, jealousies and prejudices. Elements outside our control can play a major part in our life purpose, such as, job loss, family circumstances, our environment - home or work. Factors leading to lack of security which lowers self-esteem, affecting our state of mind and confidence. We all need that feeling of security in some form to achieve our purpose in life.

Everyone has varying degrees of what makes them live their life purpose; some people want to be high flyers, live life in the fast lane socially. Others want the family to be well and safe and just to have job security and that satisfies their needs in life. To other people their life purpose is being respected and socially accepted in their community, to me this is important.

A person's life purpose should be an enjoyable experience, to feel good generally about our lives. To learn from successes and failures.

Great Men Are in History Books

Hi everyone,

Yesterday I had an enjoyable day at a local school, being a Career Coach is rewarding and it gives a great insight into a person's aspirations and dreams for the future. It is good to see a face light up when a path to their goal is placed before them. It is sad to see, the opposite end of the scale when doors and opportunities are closed.

Vince Cable has criticised the TV programme "The Apprentice" as it shows would be entrepreneurs clambering to be Sir Alan Sugar's business guru. The lies, cheating and hustle to win is basically television theatre, or is it.

Full marks for the modern style apprenticeships, a golden opportunity for individuals to be nurtured through excellent training programmes. I was speaking with Michael O'Halloran, the Sales Director for ISS, who is a major employer. Their apprenticeship programme is excellent; nothing has been left to chance. Individuals are nurtured by Senior Management and senior staff.

How refreshing to see something good and positive about business and what we now need to expect from our companies and businesses. However, we have still had to contend with egos as big as the Eiffel Tower. It is with sadness that I noticed the company, Sir Robert McAlpine, the construction company, a company who had an excellent reputation over the years being tarnished by a wrong decision by a Senior Director, who was a member of the founding family. The wrong decision was contributing to a "blacklisting "of construction workers. The company paid £220,000 to check names on the list, a list that was inaccurate but ruined several lives by its impact. Excellent trained managers do not need concocted lists to do the job. How many other "blacklists" exist in our world of business with incorrect information placed on them with a whim and a fancy!

Recently, I went to Highbury Hall, the home of Joseph Chamberlain, a prominent MP. He worked tirelessly for his people, he helped bring prosperity and commerce to his city. When he died the city, he represented came to a standstill, thousands turned out for his funeral.

So, it appears that Stephen Hester was pushed from RBS, partly his own fault. Admittedly, he did not have an easy task, but his persistent failure to not listen is not a good attribute. I was curious to know what make him "tick", what was life like at the top of a giant company. I sent letters to him by special delivery marked "PRIVATE AND CONFIDENTIAL". These letters were opened by his staff who did not understand what the words meant, or inadvertently thought they would safeguard" Hester from the outside world. Falsely, they were throwing Hester to the wrath of the public. It would be easier to gain an audience with nobility than with Stephen Hester, what is he afraid of? Why does he not allow his senior staff to discuss issues? Issues that are important to the well-being of the company. The documentary evidence, which I have seen that highlights unscrupulous management practices within the business. And until these are corrected, RBS will be the scrum of the world of banking, who unfortunately, does not even know its own company policies. The lies, the cheating, the one-upmanship, the threatening emails sent to staff, salary not paid. There is no rhythm or reason for this style of management, where even solicitors and lawyers are frightened of standing by the claimant in a court of law against RBS and the banking union run for cover. We had the reign of Sir Fred Goodwin, until he was overthrown, soon we are seeing the end of the reign of Stephen Hester, The Reluctant, who will be next to reign over the court of RBS.

There is one thing for sure, we need a leader who can speak to the people, answer the questions that need to be answered, right the wrongs that exist within its walls. Have his kinsmen who have noble skills, who have loyalty and genuinely the best interests of RBS at heart.

The Americans always like a true story of human hardship and how the hardship was overcome. Now there is an open invitation to my "friends" across the ocean to get the rights to a story waiting to be told.

Bye for now

When One-upmanship talks Rubbish!

Hi everyone,

Wow, what a life! How many times do we utter these words, I know I do, at times you wonder where people's intelligence is, or indeed what they hope to achieve. All it serves to do is to make me frustrated and angry and the speaker look completely unsociable and stupid. I am talking about the person who must have the last word, aiming to come out on top above everyone else regardless of how it makes them appear.

How many times a week are we faced with these situations in the workplace whereby logic is thrown to the wind. One-upmanship takes a few forms, firstly a question is asked, an answer is given, the answer is not believed then the "questioner" acts as if they do not believe the answer and continues to berate by asking the same question in the hope of belittling the other person in some form. As a manger I am wondering whether to install cctv cameras or hire solicitors as bodyguards in the workplace to obtain the truth, they say the camera never lies. Secondly, one of the persons blankly refuses to admit defeat in an argument and forgets to listen to their own answers. Thirdly, the person is such an authority on a subject and eager to instil their opinions on others that basic logic is forgotten.

Last week, I viewed two occasions where both persons were craving for the bright lights of fame. One person dug a hole for himself so big that I was left wondering if that's going to be our next government, I would consider immigrating to another country. Here is extracts from the conversation; "have you received your ballot paper", "yes, was the reply. ^d' When are you going to send it back?" 'I I was waiting for a phone call, which I never received" response "maybe they could not help you so that is why they did not reply". The conversation failed at good customer service and failed to help the other person. And then for an encore the person was told by the advisor to put incidents down to a life experience!

Admittedly, there are, occasions in our lives when we must put down things down to life experiences e.g. illness, breaking a bone, being ignored at a gathering. But one-upmanship is a form of bullying; it is denying the other person the human right to have a reply, the right to freedom of speech. Or worst, denying individuals help if needed and denying others the right to help.

The other incident viewed highlighted one-upmanship and complacency, an article written by a clergy man, I won't say from which persuasion. The article was about having to contend with suffering and humiliation and how we respond to them will determine both our level of maturity and what kind of person we are. Humiliation does make us deep in diverse ways. It can make us deep in understanding, empathy and forgiveness or deep in resentment, bitterness and vengeance. BUT, let's get real, minor slights individuals can contend with, but serious ones? Why does anyone have to contend with continuous harassment or abuse? Where is it written that a person can be treated as such? The clergy man continued to say, depending on which path we choose would determine our maturity and our happiness. A person deserves to be treated with respect, spoken to with respect. Anyone who thinks otherwise or places a religious angle to the argument is being complacent and encouraging humiliation and inadvertently -unchristian attitudes, the spin-offs are stupid one-upmanship in the workplace and society.

So, a word of advice, never put both feet in your mouth at the same time because you won't have a leg to stand on.

Bye for now!

Best Wishes

Age Is A Number, The Spirit Is Alive

Hi again,

Over the weekend I read with interest articles about the aging population, it made me think. There has always been varying ages in our society, nothing new, so why are politicians and think tanks e.g. The Institute of Economic Affairs obsessed with the older generation. There are suggestions that people should work longer than the current national retirement age, because mental and physical health would be heightened. Another implication is that the cost of state pensions would be reduced by people working longer. I have seen before my eyes, a politician nurturing the interest of a younger generation to obtain votes and dismissing the comment of an older person by thanking him, but he was concerned more with the views of the younger audience.

The suggestion that the retirement age be increased is good for some people, those having to continue to work for economic reasons or indeed want to for other reasons. Many who do not want to lose the daily routine of work and camaraderie of workmates. Others who cannot wait to lock their drawers, close computers and throw away work clothes for ever. But, I believe other stronger and more influential issues come into play, a major deciding factor is how older people can manage to continue to work, the type of job the individual does, the hours involved, the targets set. The main factor is the employer's attitude towards the older generation being in the workplace.

I say, the employer's attitude because, there exists managers who cannot wait to get rid of older staff, some use unscrupulous methods to achieve this aim. However, a good employer will create the right balance, utilising the "older "person's knowledge and expertise to full effect. The older person can use experience by mentoring and training younger staff in tasks and professionalism. Remember over time employees gain a tremendous amount of unwritten knowledge about the job, about customers, training requirements, and systems. At one time, it was estimated that an employee who left a business, cost that business at least E60, OOO in lost revenue. Now many, business don't take that into consideration, preferring to opt for younger staff to keep salary costs to a minimum.

It is beneficial for younger people to work alongside "older" colleagues, it gives a true reflection of society and respect for each other is brought into the workplace. It is great to see a return to the fresh style apprenticeships, both for the individual and the businesses.

It is the role of our politicians and those at the helm of industry to highlight the importance of the older person in the workplace. So, while targets and profit are important to the business, so is the human side of business important too.

Bye for now, hope you all have a good week

Best Wishes,

Anna

Les Misérables within Banking and its Duty of Care

Hi everyone, beautiful sunshine here in Birmingham today, great for the bank holiday.

Last week I hit on the topic of the culture within the world of banking, which was borne out of ultimate arrogance. Because I have worked within the private and public sector I can understand and relate to what is good and bad practice within the workplace. And hopefully through my work as a Career Coach I can bring a greater understanding and training to the working environment.

Most of us know the qualities of what makes a good leader in business, so why then is there still a tendency to allow inept "managers" to continue to destroy businesses and destroy the economic growth of the country. Duty of Care has now become a prominent subject, due to the lack of it within businesses. I have seen complacency first hand and was extremely shocked by the extent it can go.

Persons with the responsibility for staff must get to grips with what the role means. Employers have a legal duty of care to their employees, taking all steps that are possible to ensure their health, safety and well-being. Requirements under an employer's duty of care are wide-ranging and may manifest themselves in many ways. Most understand The Health and Safety at Work Act 1794, and that is the extent of their knowledge. Well. It can get even more in-depth and serious; harassment at work act 1977. Corporate manslaughter and homicide act 2007 and Breach of contract. Scary, isn't it?

All employment contracts contain an implied term of trust and confidence owed by an employer to an employee and which essentially governs an employer's behaviour towards an employee during employment. An employer must not act in a way that is intended or likely to destroy the relationship of trust and confidence between them and the employee.

So why, is it all ignored, why does this very important principle of management get rejected? It is abhorrent when it is witnessed within a corporate business, sorry, The Royal Bank of Scotland, but you have won the award again! Which only serves to highlight major flaws internally and maybe I could help Stephen Hester to right these flaws, if he wants to contact

me, I am only too willing to help!

I consider major flaws to be; where a member of staff commits suicide, ignoring staffs that are on sick leave, failure to listen to grievances and investigate accordingly and arrive at a satisfactory conclusion. False statements placed on personal files about staff. Staff placed on "action plans" with no substance, as if it was the latest fashion. Staff placed on time keeping warnings, but no record of the lateness! Yes, believe me I have seen such reports written, shocking and a disgrace to the management profession.

"Managers" who through their own egos, prejudices or whatever are willing to attack and destroy a person's character to the extreme, to destroy a person's personality, all done by "bad mouthing" the person. No thought is given as what the outcome might be for the employee or the business. I know of a Senior Manager, who realising what had taken place, announced that "there would be managers taken out and shot "if the details ever came to the attention of the outside world.

I have seen to my dismay a Senior Manager within the banking sector, sending emails to other managers to discredit an excellent member of staff, an individual who had lots of experience and was well qualified. That member of staff suffered enormously because of this manager's actions. The same manager was convinced that she could interfere in her staffs' personal lives too and promptly made a phone call to a male colleague to stop him from contacting a female member of staff, both socially and workwise. It was a wonder she was not phoning staff telling them what to have for breakfast! She did not occasions become a "temporary" doctor and offered someone tablets.

My advice is to consider your actions wisely and intelligently for the good of your staff and the business. Duty of Care is very crucial and important to your role as a manager, which is what the title means. Do not be badgered" into unlawful actions to appease someone else, think of your own self-respect and conscience.

Get to Grips with The Laws Governing Employment, You Know It Makes Sense.

Hope you all have a good week, Bye for now until next Monday.

Regards,

Anna

The Great Gatsby and The Greatness of Banking

Hi everyone, Monday is here again, a new week of dreams and hopes.

The Great Gatsby, three times that film has appeared on our cinema screens. And each time more lavish and dazzling, and the latest version iso exception, so opulent that the viewer is transfixed and whizzed into a world of 1920's parties, dancing, a world of riches and damaging corruption.

Will the 2000's be also remembered for a time of untold riches and extravagant lifestyles in The Great Banking Industry? Don't get me wrong, riches are fine, if those with the money obtain it honestly, fairly and maintain respect for their customers and staff.

I read with interest comments made by Ben Griffiths, and I wondered how much he knew of the banking industry. In his article he states the following 't recruiters report that women are telling them they do not want to work in such a nasty industry", he continues that banks themselves want to hire a range of well —rounded people with different interests outside work, they are desperate to recruit more women". My, that's sounds great for all you ladies out there.

Having seen inside the world of banking, I can understand why women do not want to enter that great domain, because basically many are lost, trapped with talents and skills that are chased underground. Lucky if a man gets on their side, or better still manage to marry a man with his foot placed on the corporate ladder.

The Great Banking is mind-blogging to say the least and once seen never forgotten. Ideas and policies are random depending on which way the wind is blowing and who is involved. The era of casino banking, the roulette wheel spins around, but who cares it's not our money! Let's have a trip to Monte Carlo, live the highlife on luxury yachts and arrive at the hotel by helicopter. Dinner is served amongst glitter and sparkle and Shirley Bassey sings her heart out to rapturous applause. A great journey for staff who, when all is said and done performed an act of good customer service. Getting carried away with the showbiz lifestyle not understanding that good customer services were part of their contract.

Back at the marble mansion, things are going askew! A customer is demanding his invoice for his leased vehicle be cancelled, because well after all he is a friend of well, you know who, the MD, without going into too much detail. Perception is important, branded about like no tomorrow, a secret code with no explanation. Staff are viewed with distain, if the dress cannot go higher to go with the heels, or she is too old then we don't want them. Never mind that the poor soul can deal with issues 20 to second, ok, maybe a slight exaggeration, but not far from the truth.

The HR department behind large desks and egos to match refuse to listen to facts, figures and demand that they know it all, when clearly, they don't and continue to slam the door.

The financial service authority tries to introduce Basel, or is it basil, no that's an herb. A manager tries eagerly to add a tone of French to the word but fails amongst fits of laughter from her staff. And Basel falls at the first hurdle, fudging figures is far easier to deal with.

Desperate attempts are made to inform the man in the black leather chair that luxurious vehicles are sitting in dealership compounds gathering dust and cobwebs, what is to become of them? sold for a profit? smuggled away? or used as a favour? who knows?

Is it the end of the "I am bigger and better than you "world of banking, or are we wondering where we are going? A little word of advice for bankers, accept that some days you're the pigeon and some days you're the statue.

"You can accept failure because everyone fails at something. Just don't accept not trying".

Until next Monday, same time, same place Have a good week.

Where is my chauffeur? Has anyone seen him/her?

Bye for now

Anna

Professional Faux Pas, Or So What, Who Cares?

The time is fast approaching for the summer holidays, thoughts of sun, sea and relaxation. Such delights create a flood of holiday expectations. All memories mingled together to give us a warm glow of well-being, excitement and hope for the future.

It would be nice to have that warm contented glow on our journeys to work each day. Currently, nostalgia is in vogue, each week there are vintage fairs taking place around the country. One local vintage fair was set up to create the 1940's, a time of war and austerity. Why, this popularity with the past? Is it to show we can pull through the recession as people did in the past? Or is it simply, very interesting and absorbing. Perhaps, is it a need to remember the days when unity existed with neighbours, colleagues and a politeness with all whom one encountered? In a nutshell.... good social values and the instilled thinking of "doing the right thing".

Thankfully, there are people of that persuasion today, but there are complacent. Dismissing the shortfalls with comments "oh well, it's the times we live in "almost to the point that everything is acceptable or equally bad "it's no use trying to put things right".I recently read an article, which shocked me, but I also know the advice to be true. And left me thinking what happened to "breaking the law". If standards were maintained, the public would not be witnessing distrust and dishonesty within the banking sector regarding the various scandals and standards of customer care would not falter.

An extract from the article written by a business guru, 'fin my experience companies can fight hard to protect key staff and an account of bullying could rebound again on you, even if you're right. It's not always a clear-cut world out there, so be careful". What a sad world we live in, in a way allowing no freedom of speech in the workplace.

Well done! To Barclays Bank last week, who by their prompt good customer service impressed a customer resulting in new business? Unfortunately, for The Bank of Scotland, they dithered so much they lost out, but maybe they weren't bothered.

This week, the faux pas for me was when Sir Philip Hampton, Chairman of RBS Bank taking part in a documentary highlighting the libor scandal stated that "the Irish love to party and no-one can party like the Irish" I don't think it was all down to the Irish, do you. By the way, Fred Goodwin is not Irish, and it was reported in the national press that he liked fresh fruit flown in from Paris, that's what I call "partying".

Talking of parties, do we get a national holiday for the Queen's Coronation Celebrations?

Bye for now, enjoy your week

Anna

Ideals Build Encouragement Opinions Can Demolish

Hi to you all, my blog is a day later due to the bank holiday and a lovely one too.

Who decided that peer pressure was a useful tool in managing staff, well, it is not, it serves only as an "opt-out" for some managers because it relieves them of their involvement in the "man management" side of the business. For the misguided manager, peer pressure comes under the banner of "empowering" staff. When "empowering "staff it was to allow them to use their intelligence and discretion when dealing with customers/clients without supervision.

I recall the time when a Managing Director of a large leasing company advised his staff that they could take it upon themselves to reprimand each other if caught arriving late for work. Wow hold on there, no way, should this practice be adopted. Don't pass the buck, that is a manager's responsibility for obvious reasons, time keeping records that might have to be shown later.

Introducing peer power opens a Pandora's Box of in-house rivalry, jealousies and discrimination for varying reasons. And the outcome, unrealistic targets set so people are set up to fail, time management concepts not understood along with other principles of good sound management thrown to one side. Nagging and apportioning blame becomes the norm, attention is not being paid to the areas where real contributions can be made, but creating an atmosphere of fear and unrest, however subtle.

Opinions and perceptions are thrown around like confetti, with no foundation or thought; reputations are destroyed, incorrect information recorded. A manager's opinion that supervisors did not even need to know about a job, if they knew how to use bullying tactics to get the work done! "Right First time" slogans branded about in the hope that it counted as management playing a part; there is no review of the situation or systems here is no positive vibes, but only serves to demotivate staff and demolish the business.

However, ideals build a business; it encourages staff to give input from their knowledge and experience. They do the job and know all the idiosyncrasies of the system. They know the weaknesses of the machines, the phone responses of the customers. They are the people to consult if you really want to do a superior quality job. Encourage pride in workmanship, as Herzberg stated, "we all need money, but real satisfaction comes from the content of our work and the fellowship we find with others in carrying it out".

Managers shape employees in their work ethics, pride, and work should be acknowledged and applauded. Encourage positive talkers, avoid belittling language or behaviour. Positive talkers use language that encourages co-operation and to defuse potential conflict. Their aim is to ensure that both sides in all negotiations win, there is no loser. Positive talkers are not content to bolster their own self-image and self-esteem but want to enrich those of their colleagues too. How many of us can say that we have truly met those kinds of people in our working environment?

Ideals come about by speaking positively, appreciating each other's goals and aspirations, being optimistic, accepting responsibility, being co-operative, saying what we mean

...telling the truth, being diplomatic and polite in doing so. Winston Churchill said, "all great things are simple", yes, if we learn to give respect, listen to each other and follow ideals to build our business.

The thought for this week "You don't have to win every argument, agree to disagree and don't believe everything you think"

Bye for now, until next time have a good a good week

Regards,

Anna

The Land of Lost Content, a Time for Reflection

Hello again from me

Yesterday I had the chance to go to a Vintage Fair and as I viewed the various objects, I wondered what stories would unfold if it were possible. Lives touched by austerity, wealth, sadness and happiness. There is a museum called "The Land of Lost Content", not only is it a museum of social history, but also a journey into personal memory, to an age of respectability, to an era of ladies and gentlemen who would be horrified at being referred to "as you Guys!"

Last week saw the closure of a well-established bakery, Hovis, operating since 1886, now hit by competition in the bread market. I wonder, if more could have been done to save the business, such as high-tech marketing and advertising. Had quality slipped somewhat and gone un-noticed, had failure to listen to and to watch customer trends played a part, had complacency crept in the back door. Who knows, but whatever, it is sad to see the demise of a piece of history.

Not too far away, is the chocolate company, Cadbury's in Bournville, a company that went through challenging times. Wise and sensible management principles and planning have seen the company through tough times. They have long seen the advantage and impact apprentices have made to the business, working on and developing some of their iconic brands, Cadbury's Dairy Milk, Bassett's and Kenco. The business has created a sustainable talent flow, with practical skills and academic qualifications. Enabling the business to produce highly skilled employees, an asset to our future and the economy.

Apprenticeships should have always been maintained, however small, it is regarded nowadays as a new concept, well it's not. Of course, now, the government is stepping in to help the cause and guide companies. Apprenticeships do help business to grow, it motivates, develops and provides a qualified workforce. Will this now discourage such comments by "jelly" brains for managers of "we can't-train everybody".... when did it all go horribly wrong? It was when people were placed in management positions by default.

Oh dear, what a dire situation to be in, Barclays Bank are introducing the '(Anthony Jenkins Project Transform" programme, aiming to renew Barclays business and reputation. Why, let your business go to the wall in the first place leading to unnecessary costs and time to turn malpractices into "new concepts" of renewing faith and trust with customers. Or is it a way of trying to prove how big bonuses are earned by the ^top dogs", running operations smoothly and intelligently means no one notices, I guess therefore, no bonus gets paid.

Congratulations to the new President of Birmingham's Law Society, Martin Allsopp. I hope he forges ahead with his plan to re-instate the legal profession to its glory days. I agree wholeheartedly with him that computers should be used by the legal profession as a tool and not a substitute for sound legal advice. Solicitors should meet their clients; nowadays there is a reluctance to do so. Cases are dealt with by "case handlers" or "paralegals". I am sure; I am not alone in requesting a real, qualified solicitor to deal with my legal affairs. How many times have you been given incorrect legal advice? I remember a solicitor requesting a payment for "thinking time", foolish me, I thought it was part of the job. There are unfortunately, solicitors who enter this noble profession, who do so solely for the monetary gain. When their upmost reasoning should be to enable justice for all, regardless of who can afford it. So, Mr Allsopp do your very hardest to bring a return to noble sense and sensibility to the legal profession, my ancestors are turning in their graves.

That's my view of the working world this week, and we seem to be shaping up.

Bye for now, until next time, hope you all enjoy the oncoming bank holiday.

Regards,

Anna

On Building A Business Relationship, The Ladder Is Slipping!

Wow, what an interesting week I had viewing the business world we contend with each day in our busy hectic lifestyle. I am not alone in my observations, such new headlines jump from the page

"church wages war on bonuses" and "bankers who presided over crash set to lose knighthoods" and "Barclays faces row over staff rewards" and sadly, the list continues whereby we are left wondering where is this huge surge for "great networking" and '{building sound business relationships" that we read about. The Royal Bank of Scotland has earned the title of "RBS half-a-job" for reasons we already know. Networking encompasses all the contacts we make each working day and can make or break a business opportunity.

On a visit to Santander to place money into my account, I was advised that I was unable to do so because it was not that type of account! Regardless, that I had in my hand a letter from Santander telling me that they eagerly wanted me to save my money with them in that type of account. I was promptly told by the advisor that she knew what she was doing and that someone else did not. The outcome was I could pay into that account, need I say more on my thoughts and views. More recently, I saw an invoice for 13pence from Isme, the catalogue people, which was duly paid. No problem, it was legally due. But view it from another angle, it sends out vibes that the company is struggling financially, it is not interested in building a business relationship with its customers. There are solicitors who refuse to take a case, under the banner of conflict of interest, but can be covering a hidden agenda, because of fear of the respondent?

How can a business carry out proficient relationship building or networking, if hidden agendas exist? Hidden agendas have always existed but have increased greatly to affect people and the business world.

A new practice of introducing 360 Feedback surveys amongst colleagues' peers is unsatisfactory and at times carried out incorrectly. The 360 Feedback is a process in which a manager receives both quantitative and qualitative performance feedback from the full circle of people with whom the manager works regularly. Great, if the people taking part are professionally trained and honest. Lombard Vehicle Management Ltd, a division of The Royal Bank of Scotland introduced this debacle and disaster reigned! Out came the knives! And lead to a torturous time for some staff, staff that had helped each other in challenging times turned into arch enemies.

False accusations ensued and turned staff eager for promotion into warrior fighters, setting out to destroy their competitors. Incidents were turned into epic proportions and ranting's commenced. Here are some of those; an email being sent from a manager "who pays your salary" to an overworked colleague to ensure that the person would be viewed in a poor light. A team manager "tearing" someone's professional letters to pieces, so the team manager's low standard of English was covered up. A member of staff complained about a manager, who had upset them to the HR department but consequently allowed another colleague (unbeknown) to take the blame. Someone reprimanded for sitting on a manger's chair, when there was no other place to sit. Interrogated by management for wishing to do a course at college! Unreasonable targets and goals set, unreasonable demands made on staff when others were allowed go on jolly" trips. A team manager commits libel by sending damaging reports to a HR department about a member of staff.

Building professional relationships did not exist within this financial environment, so how did it survive externally, it's anyone's guess.

I am hoping that the warrior of professionalism will be reign and hidden agendas of today's calibre will be reduced if not completely squashed.

Just to make you smile, a local council has issued forms to householders for completion on the subject of ('wheelie bins" for refuse collections. However, one of the questions asks what religion the householder is, now there is a hidden agenda.

Have a good week observing your working environment, until next Monday.

Bye,

Anna

Professionalism; How "LinkedIn" Are We?

What does professionalism mean in today's world? We all like to think that we understand what the term means, unfortunately it is not the case, and as always there are the exceptions to the rule.

Professionalism is the competence and skill expected of a profession, the key to quality, efficiency and raising the required qualifications. Look at the word professor, a university academic of the highest rank. The words professionalism and professor are closely linked; therefore, we have elevated expectations of our professors and professional personnel.

So, what has happened to be being professional? Has society's standard of English deteriorated so much that English comprehension has gone out of the window! We only have to read the daily newspapers and we are hit with such headlines as, "Scandal hit KPMG ", a former partner accused of dishing out secrets about clients in exchange for bags of cash and a Rolex watch. The NHS is riddled with in competencies and inefficiencies. Last week we had the story of Sir Alan Sugar facing a claim for unfair dismissal by a former employee, Stella English. Where was the professionalism shown by Stella, who claims to have been a high-flyer in the City? Sir Alan had acted professionally as proven in court, she had been re-instated, and her salary was unaffected, therefore no claim. Stella English should have known better, and her "professional "legal representative should have known better again". Did greed play a part at the expense of professionalism? Long-term this is suicide for a business, would you use the firm of solicitors she did?

Unemployment is high, economic growth is struggling; there are happy to stay on benefit. Has any government considered all the reasons why? No, probably not, not everyone is work shy. I believe that there is a problem within industry and business that needs to be rectified. People want to work for professionals in every sense of the word, would you want to work for a company that treats staff as the "low-life" or plebs? I have heard staff say, "we are only the plebs, so management are not interested in us". Tragic, but sadly true, management is there to manage the business, lock, stock and barrel, to highlight what professionalism really is.

The title management is used as a great cover —up for malpractice, dishonesty and this malpractice is hugely encouraged by the lack of professionalism. One such case springs to mind, whereby a team manager withheld an employee's sick certificate from the HR department to discredit the employee's good character, to make it look as if the sick employee had not contacted the business.

The database, LINKEDIN, brings trepidation, listed there are unscrupulous "managers" because they are given a free rein, no-one checks on their qualifications or credentials. Some claim to be able to motivate staff, if you can call motivating staff, raising a civil war within the office! Some claim to be able to turn a failing business around, when in fact; they couldn't turn a donkey around.

Disgustingly, I read "rate rigging at RBS spreads to the Far East", the Japanese regulators uncovered "seriously unjust and malicious "conduct by the bank's employees. It continues that

45

the watchdogs revealed the traders' disregard for the rules". It highlighted the bank's failure to stop the wrongdoing; it "showed serious deficiencies in its internal controls". A classic tale of professionalism, two components, of self-respect and loyalty thrown aside with no one watching.

We can travel nearer home to RBS to 't home in" on, Helen Lawson, HR Director, Group Functions and Non-Core. On the LINKEDIN website, it is stated that she shows "sensitivity" and "professionalism" when dealing with issues. She must be choosy then, because I know for a fact, that she refused to have a meeting to discuss the lack of the "Dignity at Work" Policy, and her quip remark was 'tin my opinion". She must have amazing wizard powers, to be able to form an opinion without looking and checking ALL the facts presented. Clearly, another case of the true definition of professionalism gone astray and replaced with inept conduct.

On the surface is gives the appearance that if the word "management" is used then misdemeanours is permissible in our society. Governments need to work at changing this mind-set; it is not healthy for the economy, jobs, morally and socially.

My quote for today is "Learn to listen. Opportunity sometimes knocks very softly".

Going now for my usual comforting hot latte coffee, and maybe a choc biscuit.

Have a good week, catch up with me next Monday on my take on today's world of business.

Bye,

Anna

Never deprive someone of hope, spend your life lifting people up, not putting people down

On Thursday night, I watched a programme on channel 5 pursuing the subject of bullying in schools. This weekend it was reported in the press that a boy had committed suicide because of cyber bullying. It is not the first case and only case to be reported in the press, so why is this dimension of our society treated so casually. There are teachers and managers, who treat this unsociable attribute as if it's part of growing up or part of life. Or at worst, that's it's the individual's fault, which it certainly is not. In some schools, the word bullying is not used, but used as an add-on to "keeping safe", the idea being that it's a deterrent for bullying. Does someone honesty think that the ploy works, let's face facts and reality; whatever gloss paint you use bullying exists both in schools and in the workplace.

I do not comprehend the notion that peer groups are given the responsibility of being anti-bullying ambassadors. That is passing the buck from adults to children, from management to workers colleagues. And believe me, it does not destroy the causes of bullying or intimidation but serves only to add to it.

Listen, teachers, team managers, really anyone who has the responsibility of people in "working day" situations, you have a duty of care, legally and morally. Extreme cases of bullying I believe should be considered as a criminal offence, enabling the victim to take the perpetrator to court to sue for damages. Harsh? No, I don't think so, why? Consider the child who loses their life, consider the child who sits in a wheelchair, consider

47

the man who loses his promotion and consider the woman who loses her job. Who says, now that bullying should be hidden or ignored?

I am not going to relate the signs and the remedies of this immoral unsociable condition in this blog because I have produced a CD on the subject, entitled "NO BULLYING= MORE FUN!" The CD has been designed for active interaction between the teacher and the pupils to openly discuss the problem plus I have had the opportunity to hold presentations on the topic in schools. I believe in business and education working together, therefore I cover a range of topics.

I was an associate member of the Anti-Bullying Alliance, so I certainly believe in what I say, and I hope you believe in what I say too.

Bye for now, keep smiling!

Anna

The psychology of experience and how it relates to career coaching opportunities

Career coaching is encouraging a positive 'can do" attitude instilling confidence in the aim can be thwarted, when the client had been subjected to a demoralising environment. Other factors can be the failure of the client to realise their ambitions and dreams. Failure to recognise their strengths, their weaknesses, failing to see or grasp opportunities, lack of confidence. Maybe, their energy is sapped, but should still be encouraged to take small steps in achieving their aspirations.

In career coaching terms, the mind, inner-self, spiritual, professional and environmental can help or hinder the progression.

It's down to basic steps for the client, working in harmony to see what the problem is and how it arose. Using the building-block progress, starting with the client getting to know themselves — personality, what upsets them, what makes them happy. Type of character, what skills, access to tools to achieve success, influences, knowledge of pass achievements to draw from. Working to obtain the right mix of components for the individual to increase their value and status. Helen Keller said," I long to accomplish a great and noble task; but it is my chief duty to accomplish small tasks as if they were great and noble".

Maslow's pyramid, presented as five levels, the lower four levels represents the deficiency of needs. The top level is known as growth needs. The higher needs come into focus when the lower needs have been satisfied. The hierarchy begins with the physiological needs, safety needs, the love and belonging needs, the status or esteem needs and self-actualization needs.

As human beings we have the desire to keep control over achieving a healthy independence. Every component of life is a lived experience and this knowledge increases as we progress through life.

The Simplest of Words, the Harshness of Words

Hi everyone, hope you all had a happy Easter, a wonderful occasion. It was a pity that is was the coldest Easter on record here!

Last night I watched a programme about the Bronte sisters presented by Sheila Hancock. It gave an interesting cultural view of the times. The time when language was flowery with a measure of words of self-humility. The words chosen by society were polite and sought not to offend.

I also watched the famous Oxford and Cambridge Boat Race on the River Thames in London. The BBC presenter, Claire Balding, and very good she is too, was interviewing one of the boat crews. When to my surprise up popped the caption "two times boat race winner" ...what two times! It sounds so childish, virtually, to the point of being bad English. What happened to the word "twice", or even {'thrice", (three times)? Why are words disappearing? It has been reported that words are vanishing from The Oxford Dictionary because they are no longer been spoken.

This week, in the press, Derek Sach, Head of Global Restructuring in The Royal Bank of Scotland stated that the youngsters of today can only communicate as if "texting" on mobile phones. Thankfully, not all youngsters fall into that category. But, there is a truth in the statement, has essay writing and letter writing become a thing of the past leading to low standards of English. Increasingly coupled with an aggressive tone of voice, a flippant remark, a patronising air, whichever, a person is left feeling, chewed up and spat out.

What and to whom (another disappearing word) do we blame for the demise of our native tongue? Television? Programmes like EastEnders, it's a story, make believe, actors bringing the stories to life. Not to watched and copied and re-enacted in the office the next day. Professional etiquette has also taken a dip, phrases '"thank you"; "please" gets a look of '"what planet are you on". I worked with a girl called Kiren, who when greeted with {'Good morning and how are you, she would respond "don't say good morning and never ask me how I am again. Needless, to say, no one bothered again! In the supermarket, you rarely hear the words "excuse me" when someone wants to pass, it's "I want to get in there".

I guess the list of misdemeanours is endless, my two pet hates are "at this moment in time" Oh dear, we are permanently in time, and the clocks went forward an hour this weekend. The informal words "you guys" are not suitable for a professional environment, it sounds patronising by management for its staff, and the term borrowed from another culture. Whereas it used to be "ladies and gentlemen" it is and sounds respectful to listeners. Are words disappearing because of something deeper damaging our society, the lack of God? Years ago, people added the words, "please god" to sentences. "Have a nice holiday and a safe journey" replaced with "I will".

Please God, I will have my blog next week, until then hope you all stay safe.

"The Man Who Made Time, Made Plenty'

Hi everyone, snow again! Easter is on its way, but we have the perfect Christmas card view.

My thoughts today are with Time Management, a measuring tool for the skilled manager to use wisely and sensibly. But, God help us if it gets into the wrong hands! I had the opportunity to attend the Labour Party's People Forum on Saturday at the International Convention Centre, despite the snowy conditions. And as I walked around viewing and listening to what was being said by the various VIP guests, I noticed a small table on which lay booklets about mental health in the workplace. The book gave a variety of "hints and tips" for business managers on how to spot stress, deal with the concern, basically improve the working environment in this day of targets and goals. How sad, in the 21st century that such publications must written, you would have thought that society would have improved by now. Sorry, I must not digress, my point is that some managers, not all, thankfully, think that time management is about treating their staff like micro-managed, micro-chipped cloned specimens! Managers, who confuse the elements of time management, the concept to be productive, to prioritize workloads, success goals and gain the reputation for invariably meeting deadlines. Is there enough use of technology and office equipment to save time? Ah, a faulty photocopier inevitably halts production, are there outside influences to affect production, other companies with slow recorded payment systems...that is what real time management is about.

How, in the wrong hands, time management is a dangerous weapon it can have a devastating effect on staff. It can destroy confidence, demotivate staff, it destroys personality and curbs room for growth for the business and the individual because of the constraints neither can move on, causing stagnation. Unfortunately, by unscrupulous managers it has been known to be used as a tool for bullying and intimidation, a leasing company used the time management tool in such a way, a likely contributing factor to their closure. The method used was to set timings for each task, little was known as to how timings were set. The timing was set at, say, 2 minutes, if this timing was broken by 3 minutes, the member of staff was reprimanded, and the event recorded on their appraisal to give a lower rating, hence no bonus and a down grade. Such a practice leads to the mental distress for employees, but why, is it the old story, the old bugbear of the "power ego".

Get real! Managers, YOUR STAFF ARE HUMAN TOO! Interruptions do occur, issues crop up that must be dealt with. An influx of phone calls to be dealt with. YOUR STAFF HAVE

LIVES DON'T DESTROY THEM! BE FAIR BE REASONABLE. WATCH LISTEN AND LEARN.BE LOYAL TO THE BUSINESS TOO!

By adopting the right mind-set, the business will grow, reputation will be sound, staff will enjoy going to work, will want to learn and contribute leading to togetherness resulting in excellence.

The golden rule is; "Never expect anyone to do anything that you would not do yourself"

Have a good week, until next time,

Best Wishes,

Anna

Get a return on your investments, what Grievances means

Hi Everyone, hope you all had a good weekend, and those of you who celebrated St Patrick's Day, hope you enjoyed the parades and had a brilliant day, really a day for all communities to enjoy.

"Get a return on your investment", instantly we think of monetary gain, but people are an investment too. A company employs a new employee because they bring skills into a business; they receive further training and salary. So why, are there so many tribunal cases? Why is the investment thrown away with no regard? So what changes along the way? Does having a grievance mean that the employee is no longer loyal to the business? Has the business got complacent, "No one is indispensable?"

What results in a Grievance and at worst, a situation ending in a tribunal court? It's a combination of various things. We interact with people of differing personalities, cultures, religion and skills and because of this "situations and incidents" can arise but should not be allowed to fester. The underlying problems, don't want to listen, don't want to understand, dis-interested in others, and don't want differing opinions and that destroying "power" ego.

A well-organised, employment and company policy savvy business need not worry about being judged on the amount of tribunal cases they are involved in. That is a good tip for employment hunters researching a prospective employer. It should act as a warning sign to some organisations that they are in trouble with chronic industrial relations problems and has not got the capability to resolve employer grievances.

Several Grievance cases need not end up as such, there is no need to "trump aces" or aim for one-upmanship. Or spout comments 'I I haven't got time for this", or "it's in your best interest to go away". Or the refusal of a Director of Human Resources to discuss an issue

and can only offer a dismissive statement, yes, this is another true story from RBS. And yes, throwing away a valuable investment, an employee!

If your company operates in such a manner... change it and quickly due to the serious risk to your business. Think about the consequences of taking various courses of action. In the long-term people are more interested in how management behave rather than what they say, can manage people's expectations. BE HONEST, look at all the evidence, don't be selective to suit, PROVIDE TRUST, GIVE EMPLOYEE SUPPORT, give fair criticism, give credit if due, stick to the essential arguments. Seek a result, list solutions, and implement an action plan without delay. Do not delay in making decisions; don't make a mountain out of a molehill.

Re-view your HR department, have you got the right qualified people in the roles, if disputes are not resolved and tribunal cases are increasing then no, the wrong people are in those positions.

Ask "is it worth it...what would it cost....and what would the benefits be if it proved successful to resolve".

Have a good week, keep smiling!

Bye for now.

Anna

Are we human, or are we dancers?

Hi everyone, just "nursing" a nice hot latte coffee, how soothing that feeling is especially on a bitter freezing day.

How well are we "nursed" in the workplace, what I mean is how well does our managers look after our wellbeing?

Last week it was reported in the press that there is an immense rise in the total of carers in our society and that indeed many carers must give up full time employment to carry out the duties of care for relatives. However, there are carers who with the co-operation of supportive management can continue to work full time.

As managers, we should understand that we have a Duty of Care to our staff; it does extend to issues outside the workplace without getting completely consumed by the personal lives of our staff. A little understanding for staff goes a long way in securing loyalty and ultimately raises the reputation of a company. Therefore, the actions of one manager can raise the profile of a company or tarnish it, which is an important consideration. But as human beings in an educated society we should understand people's feelings, be tolerant that our staff are made of flesh and blood and not with nuts and bolts and buttons to press.

Yes, but what about the cost to the business, I hear you ask? Ah, it's simple, if a team of people are willing to co-operate as well, nothing is lost. This basic attitude can and should be nurtured by a "real" manager, with excellent all-round management skills, which includes personnel management.

Yes, thankfully excellent managers do exist because they understand fully what the word management means.

I can give a good example from Solihull Metropolitan Borough Council. A member of staff in the Finance department had caring responsibilities for her father, who sadly suffered from dementia. But because the manager was flexible with the timekeeping, that member of staff maintained their high standard of work, meeting targets etc. the department did not suffer by the situation. That employee ensured that they made up for lost time, by starting work earlier, working later in the evening, reducing lunch time. The "real" manager did not add to the -stress or pressure that his member of staff must have been feeling. Need, I say that is why Solihull Metropolitan Borough Council has a very good reputation. Care for your staff, you equally care for your customers and vice versa.

Equally, I can highlight a company with the opposite attitude for its staff, Lombard Vehicle Management Ltd. I know, I have mentioned this company previously, but it serves only to show the difference between skilled and unskilled managers.

• A staff member requested to attend a sick relative and was caused extra stress because permission had to be sought from a few managers beforehand.

• A staff member, who had a sick relative, was interrogated aggressively by a manager on their return causing interest and amazement of listening colleagues. • A staff member had 2 days holiday entitled deducted, with no warning on their return to work after attending to a sick relative.

• A staff member who was experiencing breathing problems sent home alone

I suspect that are getting a mental picture of what it would be like to work for such an organisation, frightening isn't it, And I expect you are seeing the wider implications for this type of company and have decided which one you would prefer to work for.

When I am advising students about job hunting and interviews, I tell them that it is imperative that research is carried out to ascertain the management culture and style of a company before applying for any position.

I am so passionate about managers understanding what the title management truly means, being truly skilled and truly understand the role that they play in the business world. Oops! I haven't finished my coffee, but never mind and it is starting to snow now.

Have a good week, everyone, until next time

Bye for now

Regards, Anna

You Can't Be Serious, when did it start?

Hi everyone,

Those of you who are following my blogs each week, and thank you to those people, you will have realised that I am passionate about "doing the right thing" in business, no matter how big or small that company is.

I was horrified to read in the press about NHS staff working in fear at Adder Hey Hospital, when did this style of management come into existence? I have heard it said that the style of management comes from America, wow, frightening. There is no need for this aggressive form of running a business, there is the happy medium, you know to achieving success. This theory has been proven repeatedly and enough books written by experts in this field.

What is the root cause for this inept, inefficient and disgusting habit of having your staff work in fear, producing an environment whereby staff do not enjoy their work, have lack of pride in their work, lack of loyalty? All that is achieved is cutting corners, "fudging" figures and a workforce excellent at clock watching!

The root cause is a lack of how to manage staff effectively and efficiently, now there is people within companies who have been misplaced in positions because Managers have failed to

60

recognise their skills and knowledge. Why? Unfortunately, it is a mixture of laziness, arrogance and a lack of strong "man" management training on the part of all levels of management, from the top to the bottom.

I remember a Chief Executive at Lombard Vehicle Management Ltd when questioned about adequate staff training being introduced into the business, his reply was "we can't train everyone."

"je vous demande pardon, monsieur! it's a good job an airline does not take the same dim view on training, the passengers would have to direct the pilot, I wonder if my sat nav would work thousands of miles in the sky? I doubt it, oh dear .... Which direction to Spain?

I was horrified on Saturday to see a book for sale entitled "Office Politics: How to thrive in a World of Lying, Backstabbing and dirty tricks "by Oliver James. The book reveals the murky side of modern office life. He highlights the nasty practices that propel people to the top and shows how industries and cultures are fostering this, the book continues to give techniques on how to survive in these workplaces.

No! No, ouch! Ouch! It's disgraceful that such a book must be published in the 21st century. Come on, Chief Executives and Managing Directors clean up, sweep up; make your business well-known for all the right reasons.

Congratulations! To Land Rover, Solihull for re-introducing trainee apprenticeships, skills and untaught knowledge must be kept alive for the sake of a business.

Remember in business every management principle goes hand —in —hand, like a car with an engine; go on the motorway to a brighter future for the economy.

I am off now to enjoy the afternoon sun in the beautiful Warwickshire countryside. Until next time I hope you all have a good week and learn to breathe in your place of work.... then watch those ideas and profits flourish.

Bye

Anna

Let's Look at This Another Way

Hi everyone,

"The Road to Success", is the story of a well-known and established construction company, Sir Alfred McAlpine. The book tells the story of the early days of the construction industry. It unfolds the story of individualists, united by humour, by affection for their company, a love of their work and respect for their employees.

Can that be said, of today's employers? Realistically yes some are good, others so uncaring, it is difficult to believe. So, when did this uncaring attitude erupt? When did Human Resources treat issues as only being in black and white?

Human Resources departments, the mediator, the body of company personnel who ensured that all legalisation was updated, where fairness reigned and where an employee could run for help regarding their working environment. Grievances were investigated, on the basis that nothing was purely black and white but consisted of grey areas as well. Their role was to safeguard the employer and the employee, they had a duty of care to both and worked on the basis that bad publicity is not good for any company. And at worst, can lead to internal "corruption" amongst managers and staff.

Nowadays, how many companies do not want negative advertising? Makes you wonder, with so much bad press in recent years. The Chartered Institute of Personnel and Development, the official site for HR Managers. Their website covers all legislation in connection with employing people. I expect these trained and qualified personnel to be in corporate companies, checking that there is no room for unsolved matters, with the teaching that "people are our most important asset". Such phrases as "I haven't really the time for this "never enters their culture. Sadly, this negative attitude does exist. What is a company doing if you don't have time to review your employees' work and development? Answer is; employees are probably ineffective, and managers are not managing.

Is that the reason for the current surge of "whistle-blowers", a term I do not like, it gives the impression that these are troublemakers within a system. Basically, whistle-blowers who overall have the best interest of their "customers" at heart. Is there a chance that if HR departments listened to their staff, analysed situations, understood the implications of varying matters there would there be less of a need for whistle-blowers and the pay-outs given to them?

"Spend less time worrying who's right and more time deciding what's right "

Bye for now,

Anna

ALICE THROUGH THE LOOKING GLASS?

Hi everyone,

I have a bit of a cold today but hoping that it does not last. A big thank you to all those people who have placed me in their circles, it is appreciated.

Recently, while working on a presentation about bullying, we all know the forms bullying can take, but one that I find incomprehensible is "perceived perception". Why? because it is precisely that...perception and nothing more, it is not based on fact or on evidence. And more worrying it is creeping into the working environment.

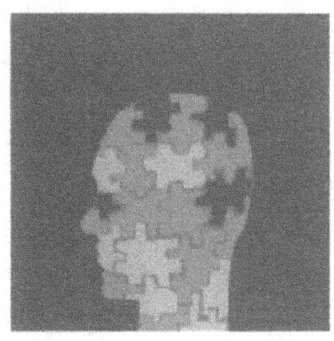

I have put on a few pounds over Christmas, does that make

Me look lazy? Mean that I am lazy? Gosh! I hope not. I know, we are prejudged, which is ok to a point. In fact, the dictionary definition of perceived perception is how someone or something is regarded in a way.

A manufacturer deciding on a new product, have a perceived perception that the public will buy it. The manufacturer will not jump head long into the venture as there is no concrete information to go on, so marketing research is conducted to give affirmation to the perception the product will sell.

Perceived perception technology is used in television studios to create the illusion a room is bigger than it is, an artistic tool and not harmful to anyone.

The harm and hurt caused by perceived perception is larger than we understand as a society. The struggles that people with disabilities have, the struggle of people over a certain age have, the perception is that these people cannot do things; they have no thoughts or feelings. So why do, supposedly intelligent people succumb to these conclusions when meeting people why? Please let me know your thoughts.

In the business world, good talent can be lost in a company because of perception. I know of a case, whereby a team manager said to a member of her staff who questioned why they were not progressing within the company. "Oh well, perception is treated very seriously in this business". This statement did not relay anything to the member of staff; it was an ambiguous statement, open to question, could be considered as bullying? And likely business ethics come into play too. The member of staff was a qualified manager, with a good reputation with internal and external customers and had an excellent social standing.

I recall working with a manager who was convinced that she knew her staff so well by just looking at them that she made the perception that one member of staff was a lesbian and that another would not be comfortable in a formal dinner jacket. She was incorrect on both counts.

Within a company and in the business world, perceived perception must be treated with a

pinch of salt. Importantly, don't judge "people" talent for your business by that method. An excellent business contract/deal is based on solid research and evidence and not perceived perception.

Until next time, have a good week and look beyond the mirror.

Zumba classes here I come!!

Bye,

Anna

Targets! Statistics! Beat the clock! Customers interrupting! Oh, what a day!

Hi everyone, it's just another day at the office for me, hope your day is going well.

Statistics and targets were always an essential element of the business world, but why have they overtaken sense ability. The elements that ensure profitability, a good reputation and excellent customer service are at times almost forgotten. Some people say, it's because society has broken down, our culture has changed; we no longer consider morals and principles. Surely. That is no excuse for the stories in the press of the horrendous treatment of patients by some nursing staff within the British NHS system. The stories would make the hairs stand up on the back of your neck, a horror story in the making. Some say, it's because God no longer plays a part in society, great was our gladness to serve God through others, for our Father taught us that all women are sisters and all men are brothers....in plain words, treat others how we would like to be treated.

The NHS is not alone, in ignoring the value of good customer service. What is good customer service? In a nutshell, it's treating people with respect, listening to people, being tolerant in dealing with a variety of people in any given circumstance. The basic component is courtesy, often taken for granted. We all like to think we have that attribute, but do we? Do we view an apology as a sign of weakness? Do we value and practise good manners? Do we view aggressive behaviour as a virtue or a vice?

Focusing entirely on statistics can lead to a host of other issues, it reduces moral amongst the staff, divides a team, limits initiative, curbs innovative ideas, difficult tasks are passed over as time consuming, so human robots are born.

Management needs to be strong in their resolve to succeed, considering their beliefs, values, what is expected and what is required of their staff, the normal everyday practices and management style. To achieve the needs of the business, three areas must be viewed and re-visited at intervals; these are organisational style, people skills and Human Resources having the "people" focused mechanisms which develop strategy. Many customer service campaigns are nothing more than "smile and have a nice day". A success story is British Airways "Putting People First" integrating actions across the spectrum of the organisation, thanks to Colin Marshall, the Chief Executive who got involved in customer service forums.

However, there is another angle too, whereby a business for some reason goes to the other extreme. On several occasions, a vehicle leasing company, part of the banking sector would not hesitate to cancel an invoice for a customer, if threatened with the words, "I know the Chief Executive, and I'm going to speak with him". The invoice would be cancelled. Can you imagine the loss of revenue and reputation to the business over time? The grapevine was in good working order and other invoices got cancelled too! Disreputable good customer service as customers were not "treating customers fairly" as was their slogan.

Don't compare yourself to the best that others can do, but to do the best you can do. If you can't be a good role model, then at least serve as a terrifying warning!

Bye for now, have a good week.

Anna

Integrity .... that's another mess avoided!

Hi everyone,

Just returned home, with a little help from the wind, from the local shops and settling to write my weekly blog.

"Never swap your integrity for money, power or fame".

Integrity, the quality of being honest and having strong moral principles, the state of being whole and undivided. Wow, the impact and meaning of such a statement, conjures images of great men and women through history. But integrity is a character trait that should be used every day of our lives when dealing with all matters, both personal and business.

Used wisely, this element is paramount in our dealings with people, today I am concentrating on how integrity impacts on a business environment. In simple, straightforward terms, treating staff fairly and being seen to do so. The result is a loyal, trustworthy, enthusiastic workforce eager to carry out their tasks, enjoying the interaction with the people they work with each day.

No doubt, most of you will have heard or seen the phase "treating customers fairly" in your place of work. As part of my management training I was taught that customers were internal and external. I firmly believe that if management treat staff, who are internal customers with fairness and integrity, then there is peace of mind and progress. Management can focus more on making the business grow and become a household name.

With hundreds of school closures and widespread transport disruption, businesses will have faced staff absenteeism during the severe weather incurring financial losses. Bearing in mind, in the UK, businesses are not required by law to pay employees who are absent due to adverse weather conditions. Many companies will have agreements, although varying, in place. Integrity, comes to the fore, making sure contractual rights and obligations are clear, fair, concise and understood. Be flexible where possible, use technology, deal with issues fairly and plan. Heed the information in the Code of Practice, every company should be familiar with this.

Reduce the stress and uncertainties for the staff, who don't forget have lives outside of the workplace, families to care for and support. Treating staff as by-products of a business, is the slippery slide to being unpopular generally, second rate and at worst closure of a business. A successful business is built on a great reputation, get things right internally, and then moving on to do the right things externally.

Last week, the Department for Business, Innovation and Skills announced new employment law changes which will affect dismissal procedures — be fair, use integrity and make sure you let all your

staff know.

This is a true story relating to a division of a mega corporate bank.

Is this integrity? To suspend an employee's salary for 10 days sick? And allow another member of staff to reach 132 days sick with no suspension of pay? Both employees were able to provide doctor's certificates. The answer is no, one employee was treated more favourably than the other.

Know the Code of Practice, understand the information, and understand the need for integrity.

Bearing in mind the need to satisfy the test of reasonableness in all circumstances, employee's records if required and relevant truthful factors.

"Discretionary", a word I am wary of, because how badly it can be handled. How is a situation judged? Will it be fair? In other words, as the saying "one man's meat is another man's poison", the deciding factor, I am sure you get my drift?

That's it from me this week, I look forward to sharing my thoughts with you all next Monday,

Bye for now,

Anna

Advertising ……. Meerkat Magic

Hi everyone, hope you all had a good weekend.

Here in Birmingham, the snow has gone, nice to see the green grass again!

What a fantastic marketing campaign for Compare the Market .com, over a million cute Meerkat toys given away to people who have chosen to purchase on their site. I wonder if the idea was the brainchild of one person or a group of people. Whichever, the result would have involved a team of people — that all important concept that strong teamwork is vital to success.

The great idea of the Meerkat characters, Aleksandr, Sergei and other family members are now related to us in a story before Coronation Street, providing an amusing prelude to this popular soap.

Marketing is a vital tool for any business and which appears to be undervalued these days. Is that why retail shops are closing? Makes me wonder. Why do they ignore the competition, which is competitive and no mistake? Why do we fail to showcase our products better, negotiate with suppliers to get the best price? Advertising that stands out from the rest, makes the consumer take note.

Coupled with pride, optimism, we need as retailers to develop the zeal; the vitality to fire the imagination to be innovative to enhance the customer's shopping experience. I remember, I know, a trip down memory lane, but we can take lessons from past, not all things are so outdated that they cannot be used or adapted to today's lifestyle. The Shop Window Dresser, remember them? Using their artistic flair and expertise to create before our eyes a window displays full of magic, be it a Christmas scene or a picnic scene in summer. It served to entice the customer into the store to experience more magic, to be lost in the excitement of looking at new merchandise, to enjoy the hustle and bustle within.

Does anyone remember Rackham's in Birmingham? Now House of Fraser. I recall a Christmas wedding window display, with the Snow Queen at the centre, dressed in a beautiful white dress, a white cloak edged with white fur and to complete the outfit a white fur hat. The groom looked suave and sophisticated in top hat and tails.

So why, cannot we use artistic talent to bring shop windows to life, highlight the products within, lure the customers to come inside, lift their spirits with a touch of sparkle and dare basically to be different from the rest.

Until next time, hope you all have a good week.

Anna

The Power of Communication

"Don't hate Mondays, you're going to spend 1/7th of your life there" (quote taken from The Daily Express). Wow, an interesting statement, what makes Mondays daunting? But why? It can be one or more reasons, traveling time, away from family and friends, no freedom to express oneself.

Do we work in an environment where we must be seen, but not heard? Do we work in an environment where a parent/child relationship exists?

Communication, working together as a team -listening, sharing, tolerance and understanding of human nature is paramount to a successful business; it also makes for an enjoyable work environment. An element that is missing or indeed frowned upon is laughter. What is wrong with sharing a joke or an amusing moment with a colleague, as human beings we need to interact with each other? I remember sharing a joke with a work colleague only for my team manage to ask in a serious tone had I been on the pop the night before or on drugs! Or the moment, they did not understand how I could find something amusing? What does someone do in such an environment? Yes, you guessed it — CLAM UP!

When someone "clams up", they are being denied the opportunity to give ideas, enjoy the office banter and basically feel part of the team. I have had the experience of working in both types of working environment, the excellent working teamwork, where daily targets were met with ease because of freedom of speech and free from bullies.

The latter negative vibes I experienced was my time working for a division of a major bank (part state-owned). I am sure you have already guessed who I am referring too. Sadly, effective communication skills were not an attribute to the business as a whole because of the bullying culture. I am puzzled at how this culture came about, was it arrogance we're untouchable? Was it Chief Executives with a gigantic ego? Is it Managers without knowledge, experience of management and no formal management training to meet the requirements of what management means?

No, this is not I believe the whole picture, it was the lack of sound, intelligent communication. The reluctance to resolve problems and issues with honesty, fairness and integrity. Sending a threatening email to a member of staff in reply to a straightforward question is not good business etiquette; neither does it resolve the matter. Neither does it show effective communication skills when a Director is reluctant to discuss a matter with a member of staff but finds that a treat is the simple answer. A Human Resources Department reluctant to talk with a member of staff but buries their head in the sand and hopes at best the member of staff disappears off the planet.

Don't get me wrong, there are excellent companies out there, corporate businesses with sound management skills, excellent communication skills, integrity, working alongside the workforce to build success.

Effective communication opens a business to success; it listens to ideas, discovers shortfalls to be rectified, listens to customer feedback, resolves internal issues fairly, and does not distort information and details to hide away from reality. Basically, a business must real and be in the real world, that does include a moral stance as well. Key notes are; preparation, gaining and keeping attention in all areas, maintaining an interest in all areas, and closing all matters positively. A happy workforce is a productive one; I know it is an old cliché, but a basic management principle.

Bye for now, take care in the snow.

Kind regards,

Anna

The importance of communication modes and concepts within NLP

Modelling, the reproduction of behaviours and beliefs of a person that has achieved success, a role model. Results show that adopting successful behaviours, language, and strategies will lead to positive changes. This method can be successful or destructive, depending how deep the role "model" ideal is practised. The client must not lose their identity and the modelling or mapping process then becomes a cloning exercise. Everyone is unique, and therefore has differing goals, ambitions, beliefs, thoughts and feelings in differing situations and environments. This is the individual's world, which must be respected, building good rapport is essential.

What we experience is represented internally in our nervous system, without being consciously aware; the five senses are constantly receiving and processing information about the world around us and the world within us. Research shows we cannot have a thought without having a physical response to that thought, be it a positive or negative.

To achieve excellent rapport with the client, excellent communication skills, a core concept in coaching is paramount to success. Communication is a powerful tool, it informs, gives guidance, educates, influences and words must be used wisely to encourage the client to reach their "pyramid". Rapport is the quality of harmony, recognition and mutual acceptance that exists with one another to encourage the free flow of communication. This skill can be learnt and used to facilitate rapport with others in any environment, even with individuals who have conflicting beliefs to our own.

The client and the coach work together to identify emotions, attitudes, body language and situations that produces negative reactions to hinder performance. Discovering the mechanics of thinking, feeling and behaviour to achieve success. The process is asking lots of questions e.g. "What exactly do they do? "How do they do it? When, where, and why do they do it? Listening carefully and observing replies and body language. In other words, getting to know the client's world, putting aside assumptions about people.

Indirect communication is subtle rapport with the client relating to voice rate, tempo, range, breathing patterns, eye contact; where the client habitually focuses when talking or thinking; when information is being filtered. The coach must not try to match gestures, but mirror by pacing verbal behaviour and sensory activity. These actions are being triggered by images, sounds and feelings related to past experiences, these can positive or negative feelings.

The outcome hierarchy is that the client acquires skills and attitudes to do what they want to do now or in the future. To think and communicate more effectively with, manage thoughts, moods and behaviours more effectively.

Business ethics for the future

Hi everyone, as I write this blog I am drawn to look out at the wintry scene. It is a magical wonderland, filled with memories of childhood, building snowmen and sliding downhill deciding who could go the furthest... being sent home early from school because of the snow ...happy days!

But those are only a few of the memories of school days; the list is endless to a degree. Another aspect of school days comes to the forefront of my mind, the principles and moral ethics which we were brought up to respect and apply in our daily lives.

Last week, in a national newspaper I read the astonishing news that children will be taught how to manage their finances, how to invest wisely, which is a sensible idea, nothing wrong with the concept. What I find astonishing and concerns me is the financial institutions that have been chosen to carry out this important task. Firstly, one of these institutions, partly government-owned because of their mismanagement of financial affairs has been considered for guiding our future generation in management of money and assets. Secondly, it has been reported in the press that Fred Goodwin is being sued by shareholders for failing to curb financial losses. Surely, we want our children to be taught by companies/financial institutions with a sound and professional reputation which our children can respect and admire.

The "teacher" tasked with this important job should be assessed for their ability, moral, ethical and professional fairness towards their customers and indeed also their staff. And there lays another tale to tell.

What is your thought? I would be very interested to hear from you.

Bye for now, watch for my next view on the business world next Monday. In the meantime, take care out there.

Best Wishes,

Anna

Making Your Voice Heard... won't someone listen?

I'm worn out; no-one is listening to what I have to say! Everyone is jostling to be heard, I am afraid of being overlooked, made to look insignificant in the eyes of my colleagues.

Making your voice heard should be simple and straightforward, at times it is a challenging task. Does it seem that your business is always listening to the same people?

It is important to be heard and listened too for your health too as well as progression in your career; we are human beings, not throw away wrappers.

First and foremost, you must be valued in the business, as I discussed in April's article. There are many considerations before voicing opinions, are your views consistent with the views of top management. It is important to recognise the relevance of the questions and to know the answers to them. Of course, there are difficulties that can be encountered on the way, the unwillingness to change, vested interests and the dampening force of the bureaucracy.

Influence and power are nothing more than the potential to get things done, making your voice heard is central to acquiring influence. If we use influence ethically, it is a powerful skill in life and in an organisation. Make sure you use what influence you have for the good, to benefit people and not the reverse. If an organisation allows "the reverse" then consider your own mission statement. To know if you have influence, I have a simple questionnaire that you can complete, and forms part of knowing yourself.

There are three steps to being heard, communication, recognition and influence. There are eight steps to successful communication. All based on clarity, the appropriateness, the delivery of the message. At school I remember the teacher teaching us "big" words in vocabulary and hoping that we use them at every opportunity. On the other hand, at work I was advised not to use "big" words because some staff might not understand the meaning, has the standards declined or is it a stance for plain language?

Recognition; remember that you want to be taken seriously, is your talent being recognised, if not, why not. Ego is a positive tool, but do not let it take over at the wrong time. Image determines preferment or promotion based on performance and exposure. Give the matter of image the priority it deserves; how you dress, are you confident, what you sound like and say. Make the most of what you have achieved and look for opportunities to build on your image and skills. Being heard in your job appraisal is very important too, do not become a "skill-tap" turned on and off by management, it is your chance to be heard. Good managers will recognise this fact and listen to your story and will match your talents to the job demands.

Win hearts, then minds, be enthusiastic and Be Yourself

Can I do it? I don't know, yes, I can do it!

Increasing your value and selling yourself in the Workplace

The concept is alien to us when we think of ourselves as a commodity to be sold. Yet, in some areas of our lives we do it without thinking. Going out for the evening, we dress up. Preparing for a dinner party is all about doing things to create the right impression.

The workplace is no different, successful people "sell" themselves, look at celebrities; they "sell" their concepts, ideas and beliefs. The key to selling yourself is not to cross over the fine line to being arrogant. There are three factors to avoid doing this, don't be a "clever beggar", and even though you could be right, people don't like this trait and can cause you problems along the way. Secondly, the goodwill, favourable opinions and endorsements of others is important to showcase your ideas. Understand that goodwill is paramount; ideas can be stolen and claimed by others. Thirdly, you must almost get into the mind-set of the listener, know about him or her, their attitude, their response and what they want to hear. In short, to get others who have reached the top to want to take on board your ideas and concepts? Warnings, thread carefully, don't overload ideas, and present it to the right person at the right time. It is not an easy task, juggling with other people's insecurities, our own insecurities, our culture and our own beliefs.

You need to be committed to yourself and your success, regularly monitor your successes and failures. Be realistic in your efforts and make the right career/job decisions involving your progression, of course this will be dependent also on your circumstances and family commitments. Make a positive effort to see yourself as others see you, reply on people who will be honest, without being cruel, and have the desire to be objective.

Increasing your value relates to other people recognising your worth and giving you credit for your achievements. View the company's mission statement, their employee relations, and employee care and employee development, what is the reality. Write your own mission statement, how it compares. Do you "fit" with the organisation? Great if you do, if you don't then reconsider your choice.

Self-development is about continuing education and learning, so look, learn and listen. Not just in the workplace but outside too, take a wider interest in the world, be involved, and be interesting to be valued. There are the "do's" and "don'ts" to be taken into consideration when assessing your value and worth to a business. If you want to find out more about these factors and how I can help you achieve your value in the workplace, please contact me.

Each coaching programme is individually designed to suit the individual's needs and circumstances and in strict confidence and code of ethics.

Remember! Nothing stands still, if you are not increasing your value, then it is likely your value is being eroded, put a stop to it now, I can help you.

If you have the capacity to innovate you should recognise that you have the responsibility to put your talent to beneficial use.

Increasing your value in the workplace, increases your value to yourself, the outcome is a lot of personal satisfaction.

A few years ago, I attended a conference, the speaker said that it was impossible to be a success outside work and be a failure inside work, how true that is.

Next month, watch for "Making Your Voice Heard".

By Anna Kelly

"You're Like Your Father!" But How Well Do You Know You?

How many has those words been spoken to people, yes, of course we are going to inherit traits from our fathers and mothers. We also carry our own characteristics that make us individuals, hence our own identity.

In choosing a career you need to know the type of person you are, your personality type. The key steps are what you are, what you want to put into life, what you want from life, the aspects and why. When you have decided those values, look at your personality type, are you assertive, passive, aggressive, gregarious or introverted. List your strengths, hopes, fears, insecurities, interests and your reaction to risk, failure, challenge and pressure. You need to know how ambitious you are and how to identify your aspirations in life.

To achieve the right balance and your goals in life. You must balance three areas of the body. The head (intellect), the heart (emotional responses) and our hands (practical output). It is a sad fact that many people have not assessed those areas and have become frustrated and unhappy, and left with a feeling that their worth is not recognised in the workplace or indeed personally.

Whatever career path anyone chooses, everyone needs a sense of fulfilment, satisfaction, to be able to use skills and abilities. For others a challenge spurs them on, the exhilaration of achievement. So, do you want to "do something" or "be someone"?

Your answers to the questions are important, understanding each element, learning to recognise an opportunity and grasp it. Missed opportunities are experienced by us all; trying to keep them to a minimum is the important.

Being a success is a wonderful feeling, it boosts your confidence, it invigorates you, and it encourages you to do more in life, both personally and in your career.

Anna

People Are Our Most Important Asset, Majority of City Firms Struggle to Fill Vacancies.

In a recent newspaper article companies claim to struggle to fill vacancies, the cause being blamed on a shortage of skills. The underlining factors are management indifference to quality training and staff. Why such indifference in industry? Surely success is paramount in terms of achievements and reputation. Has arrogance and one-upmanship taken over. I was shocked to hear a CEO of a leasing company say " we cannot train everyone", so how was the decision made as to who should be trained. I hasten to add that that business is no longer in existence.

Badly trained staff, lacking knowledge and skills move on to other companies taking those lack of talents with them. The lack of knowledge is not improved on and so nothing changes. Skilled people spread their knowledge so industry grows, but only if the talents are recognised by their employers. I have been annoyed and stunned recently by a paralegal's lack of understanding of the term "a conflict of interest" and the distinct lack of customer service skills. Excellent customer service skills are not confined to the service industries. The legal profession was always highly respected and held in high esteem. I sincerely hope that legal knowledge and training is not going down the slippery slope to disaster. I will not be recommending that firm of solicitors to friends or foe!

On-line application forms are not wholly satisfactory, success is based on entering the right "buzz" words on the application. A computer cannot highlight character and personality traits and misses the overlap of skills. Unfortunately, people end up on the wrong career path for assorted reasons, financially, personally and maybe given the wrong career advice.

Career advice in schools and colleges is patchy, basic information is given, but the vital information that is needed is missing. The information that carries an individual through life to achieving their dreams and goals are missing. Everyone should be allowed that basic right to achieve what they feel comfortable achieving. That is where my skills are honed to coach individuals to open that door to their working life and embrace the challenge.

Along with a company's training policy or lack of, culture, communication and opportunities ethics. A business can destroy itself without even realising it. Reputation, the gigantic billboard to the world can be pushed aside. Senior managers can only focus on profits and statistics, but who fail to discover that people talk. Customers, past employees can voice their praise or discontentment. Reputation can be gained or lost. Let's be honest, who would want to be employed by a company not respected in the world of industry and business. I know I can name a few, can you?

Bye for now until next time,

Anna

Is It Pride, or Am I Proud? Learning to speak the language of success!

Have you ever thought about our language, have you noticed how it is influenced by other countries? It has absorbed a richness enhanced by the Normans in 1066, the French and the Greeks. The seafaring sailors introduced "sayings" to our shores such as "the exception that proves the rule" and cheap at half the price". English is by far the most widely used official language in the world, and English has the widest vocabulary in the world. Today it is influenced by the American English language, words are taken from the latest films or television series, words such as awesome and wicked. The word "wicked" has been turned on its head! It now means something, or someone is good

I remember at school, the teacher spending valuable time teaching us "big" words for the future, unfortunately it appears this is now lacking today. Most of us have our pet hates we come across every day, mine happens to be "this moment in time" why? Because what else are we in only time, apparently the phase was introduced into vogue by a politician stalling for more time to answer a question, but who knows

However, nothing can beat good clear, concise communication, using language correctly in all job applications is paramount. It goes without saying, but you would be surprised at the level of bad English used. Childish English from a university graduate does not give a confident impression to a future employer, but I can assure you it works both ways. An incident comes to mind when an employee used the word "parallel "and the

Managing Director asked him what it meant! Ok, it was either a test of the employee or sarcasm by the MD, but nevertheless not a good management tactic.

Why suddenly the trend to follow a sentence with a string of exclamation marks!!!!!!!!!!!! See what I mean, one exclamation mark is the correct form and quite sufficient. The latter is aggressive and overbearing.

In a professional workplace project positive expectation, speak clearly, concisely become a positive talker, speak honestly but choose your words carefully, do this by placing yourself in the position of the listener. Express appreciation, express responsibility, and speak as a team player.

Excellent communication skills lead onto good manners, knowing how to act in a professional environment. Simple things like getting peoples' names right, using polite terms e.g. "thank you" and "please". In interview practice sessions, it is amazing how many people find it difficult to shake a person's hand on meeting. Remember a good handshake tells a lot about a person's character too.

A CV IS ABOUT YOUR LIFE, MAKE IT YOURS FOR LIFE.

Until next time, good luck job hunting.

Regards,

Anna

It's Effective, It's Reliable, It's Quality, It's Professional Etiquette

"Paul's professionalism, enthusiasm, attention to detail and an understanding of our working environment was outstanding".

Paul is not alone, but we need more people like Paul in every sector of business. Focusing on delivering the best possible customer service is the most effective way to build trust and maximise the opportunity for growth. Excellent customer services should travel throughout the business, gathering along the way the workforce, all working together in a professional manner. We spend a great deal of time in each other's company, so why not make it work.

Listening and questioning are paramount to any good working relationship. Ignoring professional etiquette can leave reputations broken and destroyed. All training should be implemented and tailored to ensure development, seeing, hearing and feeling the commitment of the workforce and the business hierarchy.

Respect allows good people to disagree without animosity, different people react to pressure in diverse ways, accept that no-one is perfect, and anyone can have a difficult day. Be realistic! Help them, be ready to jump in to help when necessary. Honesty, integrity and patience are probably under-valued but vital for good working relationships. Compromises cannot happen without understanding the other's point of view, how often this factor is forgotten in the quest for one-upmanship. To maintain productivity and to prevent morale decaying, conflict needs to be resolved swiftly and effectively, create a win win situation.

Understanding professional etiquette means maintaining a strong and confident demeanour for others to see, hiding worries and concerns. It relies on building an inner strength to remain positive with yourself and a persistence to keep going when under pressure. Please do not forget the tonic of a sense of humour

Without professional etiquette a business will fall like a house of cards, lack of clarity about objectives, useless questioning, and failure to be polite in all transactions. Processes not recorded, deadlines missed and reports missing. Influenced by the wrong people, ignoring common sense.

Professional etiquette is for life in all situations and can be learnt, learning how to cope with criticism, conflict and difficult conversations is not to be disregarded. Until next time, wishing you all a Merry Christmas and a Happy New Year

Anna

So, What Can You Do? Why Throw Your Skills Away?

Why? A strong valid question, I am sure you will agree. So why in recent months are people being advised precisely to do so? Who are they trying to please? Surely not themselves, "selling" themselves short in skills and talents is lowering confidence and self-esteem.

I am shocked to hear from clients that they have been advised by "advisors" to disregard qualifications obtained because it was obtained too long ago. To tailor their CV to the job to which they are applying for, yes, BUT within reason. In other words, you don't eliminate skills and talents.

To obtain qualifications and skills people have worked hard, tears have been shed, frustrations overcome to learn new skills. So, how dare anyone say "destroy" them, to banish to a back drawer a crisp quality certificate with an Examining Board and College logo emblazoned on it.

Now, let's get to the reality of the matter, your CV is about YOU, your working life and therefore your CV should be individual to you. It should not read the same as your classmates or work colleagues.

Your prospective employer should be interested in you, what you have achieved. Your prospective employer should be skilled to assess the qualities and skills required for the position advertised. Unfortunately, if a company/business does not know and must be "spoon-fed" then they are on the slippery slope of going out of business. Hence candidates are being asked to write several varying CV for varying positions basically not an ideal situation. No excuses acceptable either, a company's HR department should also have the professionalism and skills required to do the selection process. At the end of the day, it is not out of reach.

And, yes, your employer does need to see the dates that you were employed, again it tells them about you. If dates are missing, what signals are you sending to the interviewer? Remember, gaps in your CV raises questions, unnecessary questions and remember your CV is about YOU.

Next month I will be viewing language used in presenting the best CV possible. Suddenly, I am thinking why people now place a row of!!!!!!! (Exclamation marks) after a sentence. Is for effect or spoiling for a fight with the recipient!!!! (Oops! It can be catching).

Until next month, good luck job/career searching.

Anna

Increase Your Value

Can I do it? I don't know, yes, I can do it! Increasing your value and selling yourself in the Workplace

The concept is alien to us when we think of ourselves as a commodity to be sold. Yet, in some areas of our lives we do it without thinking. Going out for the evening, we dress up. Preparing for a dinner party is all about doing things to create the right impression.

The workplace is no different, successful people "sell" themselves, look at celebrities; they "sell" their concepts, ideas and beliefs. The key to selling yourself is not to cross over the fine line to being arrogant. There are three factors to avoid doing this, don't be a "clever beggar", and even though you could be right, people don't like this trait and can cause you problems along the way. Secondly, the goodwill, favourable opinions and endorsements of others is important to showcase your ideas. Understand that goodwill is paramount; ideas can be stolen and claimed by others. Thirdly, you must almost get into the mind-set of the listener, know about him or her, their attitude, their response and what they want to hear. In short, to get others who have reached the top to want to take on board your ideas and concepts? Warnings, tread carefully, don't overload ideas, and present it to the right person at the right time. It is not an easy task, juggling with other people's insecurities, our own insecurities, our culture and our own beliefs.

You need to be committed to yourself and your success, regularly monitor your successes and failures. Be realistic in your efforts and make the right career/job decisions involving your progression, of course this will be dependent also on your circumstances and family commitments. Make a positive effort to see yourself as others see you, reply on people who will be honest, without being cruel, and have the desire to be objective.

Increasing your value relates to other people recognising your worth and giving you credit for your achievements. View the company's mission statement, their employee relations, and employee care and employee development, what is the reality.

Write your own mission statement, how it compares. Do you "fit" with the organisation? Great if you do, if you don't then reconsider your choice.

Self-development is about continuing education and learning, so look, learn and listen. Not just in the workplace but outside too, take a wider interest in the world, be involved, and be interesting to be valued.

There are the "do's "and "don'ts" to be taken into consideration when assessing your value and worth to a business.

Remember! Nothing stands still, if you are not increasing your value, then it is likely your value is being eroded, put a stop to it now.

If you have the capacity to innovate, you should recognise that you have the responsibility to put your talent to effective use.

Increasing your value in the workplace, increases your value to yourself, the outcome is a lot of personal satisfaction.

A few years ago, I attended a conference, the speaker said that it was impossible to be a success outside work and be a failure inside work, how true that is.

The Covering Letter

The words "covering letter" sound almost dismissive, just a letter that is attached to the vital CV to state the applicant's name, address and why the position is sought. Mainly, the contents are bland and uninviting and set to a format churned out by school leavers and job seekers alike.

The covering letter is far more important than it is regarded; it is a window to a person's skills, talents, personality, work ethics and character. I guess it can be considered as the

X-Factor on paper; the applicant wants to capture the interest of a future employer. To write a noticeable covering letter the applicant must have a keen sense of what makes them unique as an individual.

As a career coach my role is to inspire and guide people to consider their future by exploring innovative ideas and learning about their own talents and character.

The basic rules apply;

• Why do you want the position, be natural and realistic?

• What you can offer the company, tailor the skills and competencies to match the job role

- Something positive you have learnt about the company

- Conclude by thanking the company/business and hope to meet soon

- Remember! Good spelling and communication skills are a key to success

Have you lost your way on your career path? Made redundant and want to explore innovative ideas. Not being as successful as you had hoped in the workplace. What can be done to ease the pressure and restore your confidence in these situations?

Next month I will give an insight into the working environment, what employers are grasping to get from their workforce and equally what employees are grasping to get from their employers.

Searching for a Job……the Working Environment and the Expectations

Making the transition from education to work can be daunting for some, indifference for others. The working environment varies from one company/business to another based on the office culture formed by the company. Learn to understand if the culture fits comfortably with your own work ethics, ideals and principles.

The employer/employee relationship is a two-way process, comprising loyalty, honesty, and professionalism always in dealing with internal and external customers all wrapped up in a Duty of Care.

Professionalism is being polite, courteous and respectful when dealing with work contacts throughout the day. Each employee represents the company; they become the company when dealing with customers, manufacturers and suppliers. Appropriate time keeping, excellent teamwork qualities, using the skills and qualifications as stated on your CV and the eagerness to learn new skills and processes are part of the package too. Eagerness is linked to enthusiasm, a valuable attribute to success but an attribute that can be destroyed by a bad employer.

Employees expect some of the same qualities from employers, together with fairness and the opportunity to progress and learn.

Be realistic in what you expect from your employer, but also be realistic in what your employer expects from you, the employee. Such as targets attainable and the hours to be worked.

The more the new employee learns about their personality, character traits, knowledge and expertise, the more they understand what they have to offer employers and what they expect to achieve.

Never lower your ethical or educational standards to "fit in" with a company. If you must do so, then re-consider your position. I know of an incident when an employee at a major bank was asked to lower their standard of the English language as some staff would not know the meaning of "big" words.

Coaching models

More than one hundred coaching models have been published, so the role of a career coach is diverse and unique. This also shows how the client's coaching programme can be adapted to suit their requirements, keeping in mind the obligations and professional guidelines required.

The coach must understand the client's life purpose, their cultural, social and religious beliefs. These factors all have a contributing effect in the workplace and the coaching model used. The coach should begin by setting an agenda, a coaching model which suits the client's long-term expectations, keeping a balance between desires and the achievable. The coach and client should have an in-depth discussion to develop the coaching model, discussing strengths and weaknesses, the reasons for both, setting tasks and goal setting — the coach facilitating the resources. The client must have the ability to self-manage their coaching programme; the coaching programme must be monitored, using the life purpose statement and tasks completed as the benchmark.

The elements are major factors; the client must know their capabilities, personality character traits, which people do they relate to and what situations they feel at ease.

Behavioural change can affect the coaching programme; this can be impacted by a change in working environment, organisational bullying and colleague problems. These negative vibes cause problems for the client, the coach must plan an effective training model to restore confidence and facilitate the success of the programme. Having a strong ethical relationship with the client means the client can share their problems with the coach to identify the root cause. The client's ideas or hopes can differ from the organisations, can be difficult to resolve, but this is where the skill, knowledge, negotiation skill and internal professional contacts of the coach come into play. Sometimes organisations do not have man-management/personnel skills to get to know staff, therefore all the attributes of a client's ability or personality is not seen. These attributes are known as overt, open for all to see and covert, not openly displayed.

By being objective about the root causes of problems, setting cognitive based tasks to reach goals will bring positive changes and is a holistic component of the programme-

Education; Robust or Destructible, Can We Use Our Own Intelligence and Initiative

Weather-wise, we cannot complain, temperatures are high for this time of year. But for many of us will our temperatures rise to hear that seven-year olds are to sit exams, to access their intellect and their ability to learn.

This plan is flawed, firstly because children differ, some are confident, some lack that quality and display an intense shyness. Unfortunately, shyness can be regarded as being stupid by some teachers and therefore the child is targeted with that title for years to come. Secondly, children learn at different speeds and should not be degraded at the tender age of seven! In fact, individuals develop at all ages, some do not become academic until they have left school. I coach people at all levels and ages, so I know first-hand that people cannot be placed so easily in pigeon holes. I explain in coaching sessions that shyness can hold people back, but with the right training methods this debilitating social trait can be overcome

Surely, everyone knows that up to the age of 11 are informative years, where learning should be fun, interesting, exciting, really a time for exploring and adventure. The three "R's, reading, writing and arithmetic the highly important basis of a child's education.

I am surprised that parents are putting up with such treatment of their children. Children need to feel safe, secure and protected, this importantly is a parental duty. Teachers have a strong duty of care towards their tiny charges, and most teachers respect and accept that responsibility.

It appears the government grasp a bit of an idea and run like mad with it, but do not see the full picture or the consequences of their actions. Children in China are subjected to a stringent educational system from an early age. We read reports in the papers about Chinese children committing suicide because of the pressure. We certainly, do not want that culture emerging here, so why is teachers not speaking out against these plans for children in this country.

Today, we read that teachers are leaving the profession for pastures new, there is a shortage of supply teachers. I am not surprised, teachers are demanded have a finger in varying pies, from teaching, nanny and clerical duties. Ticking boxes right, left and centre all supposedly in the interest of progress, in my book it is half a job most of the time. Teachers checking children's' lunch boxes and confiscating chocolate, food that teachers deem unfit for human consumption. Get a grip! Teachers are there to teach, to encourage intelligence and initiative not to stand guard on lunch boxes. Let parents be responsible for their children's welfare by allowing them to use their intelligence and initiative as adults.

We have all heard the phase "an Englishman's home is his castle "(refers to any nationality) and so it should be. So why then, are we bombarded with "cold calls", I received four today. Cold callers are not invited to phone us, they are intruding into our lives, our private domain. These "cold callers" act as if we should not object, but instead be delighted to spend our money with them or be excited to answer customer surveys. Cold callers are an apt word, they are cold in attitude, putting sales above what might be the situation in someone's home.

The power of the Nanny state is going overboard; we get bombarded with invitations to go for various medical tests, not one letter but a string of letters, like fan mail coming through the letter box. Letters with the large insignia of NHS blazoned across the envelope for all to see. There is so much money wasted on useless letters being posted, charities must waste loads of money with appeal letters ending up in the waste paper bin. If the public want to contribute to charities, they can use their own intelligence and initiative to do so.

The government urge to tell us what to eat and what not to eat, informing us that one minute something is bad for us, then saying it is healthy for us! Dementia testing being introduced with no cure for such a tragic upsetting illness. We are told that it enables people to then change their lifestyles early to get ready for the outcome. Surely, life is for living and to be enjoyed to the full. If we fail to allow that, then why be born at all.

Recently, Saga Insurance sent out four letters to an individual trying desperately to retain the customer. Could this be classed as a form of bullying by a company, one wonders or was it a lack of intelligence on their part.... A waste of postage costs and initiative.

A missed dental appointment gives way to a bombardment of phone call from the dental surgery, what happened to the time when a re-appointment letter would be sent. Are we being denied a bit of freedom to use our individual intelligence and initiative?

A story once told, of an old lady who walked with a limp, the ladies copied, and it became known as the Grecian bend. Like sheep they followed, ignoring reality because each lady wanting to be fashionable. They failed to use their individual intelligence and initiative.

Tunnel vision never achieves anything, but using intelligence and initiatives increases success

Are the Bandwagon Wheels Falling off Career Coaching?

I have been astonished by the "expert" career advice being given to students, a mix of advice, some good, and some bad. Suddenly, various charities and organisations are claiming to be specialists in this area of knowledge. I am a qualified Career Coach and I really enjoy going into schools to conduct mock interviews, imparting knowledge and superior quality advice on applying for jobs/careers for the present and for the future. But at times I am disgusted by the lack of professionalism that I see amongst the "interviewers". Usage of mobile phones, texting as if their lives depended on it, the failure to greet other "interviewers" on meeting, to setting up ridiculous stunts to catch the poor student out. That is not the intention of mock interview sessions in schools, and unfortunately arrogance shines through like a beacon, sending out negative signals to students.

Why the mismatch of volunteers? Qualified and unqualified Surely, the plan is to educate students on the skills required to obtain their dream jobs.

There is a lot more to career coaching than meets the eye, initially it is about the person getting to really know themselves, believe me that is not as easy as it sounds. These "experts" tell students to go online to complete personality tests to find out about themselves. This notion might help to a small degree, but underlying skills and talents do not shine through. So, these tests in practice are useless, I liken these tests to the "fun "personality tests featured in glossy magazines.

Many companies are now organising "help in the community "schemes and releasing staff to attend these sessions as "interviewers". No doubt some will be really interested in the scheme for the right reasons. Others will see it as an opportunity to further their own careers and for some it will be a day away from work. Everyone is joining the bandwagon, the Catholic Catenians, a social organisation for men, who incidentally claim to be "proudly" Catholics are now trying their hand and there of course lies another story too. The organisation is not a charity as we envisage, but they do fundraising.

I am a Career Coach and my big concern is that these sessions will provide varying pieces of knowledge depending on the "interviewer". I strongly believe and know that career coaches offer a greater insight into the working environment and how to achieve real success.

I can open the door to any business without stepping inside the reception area that is just one of the skills I can offer. Recently, I viewed examples of CVs' online offered by these "experts" and unfortunately the standard falls well short to ensure employability.

So why are schools not using the skills and knowledge that is provided by career coaches, I have a passion to do things right, every coaching programme is unique to the individual. Therefore, each CV is unique to the individual, talents, skills and knowledge previously untapped is highlighted.

The government still claim that students are lacking in the basic interview techniques, the stories I am told by businesses is amazing. Students turning up for interviews with bad attitudes, unprepared and disinterested on all levels. So why are schools still following a scheme that has shortfalls? My advice to everyone looking for a career or job is get good coaching for now and for the future.

Primary level of coaching and how core coaching skills relate to this area of work

Primary level of coaching is the recognition of maladaptive behaviour and emotional patterns, meaning the client is not

adjusting to the environment or situation; this can lead to psychological problems and associated behaviour and actions. The coaching approach is cognitive, acquiring knowledge and understanding about the client, hidden and open attributes. A constructivist approach to overcome the consequential behaviour of negativity, focusing on replacing these negative thoughts and behaviour with more acceptable and realistic thoughts.

Core coaching skills are in focus for the coaching to be successful, being good conversational skills, non-judgemental communication, displaying empathy with the client with the use of facial gestures, body language, eye contact and mutual respect.

Primary coaching, not related to identity or belief systems, designed to suit the client, is not interpretive or motivational but behaviour and performance changing, the factors are; observational data, action and task orientated, problem solving to prioritizes aims and goals.¹

The coach ascertaining what the underlying problems are, if any, has hindered the client in the past or will in the future. Subtle differences between the direct approach and the conventional directional coaching will dependent on the coach's methods, a mixture of both methods could be used if necessary.

The direct approach is solution focused-coaching, the question is outcome centred placing the onus on the client to make decisions, to perceive the future without the problems. Asking the client what changes they wish to make, how they will know when the coaching has been successful and has the main issue ben addressed, if any exceptions.

Directional coaching is past problem related coaching and client decides the duration. The coach asks the client how they can help, encourages the client to discuss and probe deeper to vocalize the problem, ascertaining the underlying or hidden factors.

Using the life purpose client assessment set the time frame, the standard. Identify the goals to be achieved. It is important to set the right tone of respect, enthusiasm, the right atmosphere to encourage ideas., addressing the key issues of cognitive and behaviour patterns. Discovering fears, problems, frustrations and ways to overcome them. Re-assessing the progress, consistent and regular monitoring to readjust goals and behaviour patterns if necessary.

Enabling the client to be positive, overcoming problems by planning, new skills training, researching the availability of resources. Assisting the client to be more self-observant of their interaction with colleagues, but not doubting their own ability.

Help the client to vocalize, using narrative techniques understanding the differences between experiencing something to relating that experience to a third party. Workplace changes, culture, values, management style, job roles, skill levels, staff behaviour all influence the client. The coach helps the client alter perspectives on events by visual imagery, verbalizing visual sequences from specific experiences, thus making conscious changes. Asking the client – why they think they are suffering? How it has changed them? Could they put it into a story to convey the key elements?

Secondary level of coaching and how core coaching skills relate to this area of work

Secondary level coaching covers deeper issues of motivation, personal beliefs and drivers of behaviour. To uncover contributing factors in the client's subconscious that influences expectations both inside and outside the working environment.

The subconscious mind can hold thoughts of irrational beliefs, neither logical nor reasonable. Often attributed to an incident affecting the client dramatically. Psychologist Albert Ellis suggested three steps to discovering a person's beliefs. Activating and recording the event leads to emotional responses or maladaptive thoughts, being the objective situation. Beliefs; the client records negative thoughts as they occur. Consequence; negative thoughts and ensuing behaviour are identified, the connection between them explored. Working on the findings to adopt new belief systems and action the changes needed, called reframing.

Excellent communication skills, empathy, non-judgemental, to encourage and methodically lead the client to be open with their thoughts and feelings, however painful recalling the past or present. Understanding what influences the client's behaviour in the workplace and how expectations are affected. In practice, focus on beliefs, assumptions, motivational factors. To re-interpret and contextualize the past to accentuate the future and changes that will occur. Raising awareness, confidence, and self-evaluation will improve positive belief systems in the subconscious mind.

There is no guarantee of success in the workplace, the client can learn from the past by planning for the future, realistically exploring other avenues. Setting expectations too high, focusing only on goals can have a negative outcome. Impeding flexibility, creating rigid goals lead to a closed mind for change, limits choices and optimality achievements. This frame of mind often presents unfounded anger and overt independence, equally if the organisation relies on analysing and creating an atmosphere of pressure this results in negative reactions.

Negative emotions, thoughts and feelings, worrying about other people's perceptions can lead to non-acceptance of self, lowering the immune system, depresses mental and physical function and capability of achieving goals. Positive emotions have the opposite effect and the brain works in a balanced mode which is conductive to change.

Visualization helps deal with problems by using imagery. Using the left logical side, and the right creative side of the brain. Logic and creativity are linked to create imagery to change emotions and feelings, turning into physical sensation, these positive images can relieve or eliminate the symptoms of problem areas.

Visualization techniques are relaxed, quietly choose an image, unique to the client and easy to recall. The client pictures the image, places themselves in the role, hear themselves speak, seeing themselves performing the chosen role. This is a good homework task, it helps the achievement process, encourages confidence, self-belief and motivation.

The client needs support from a mentor, preferably someone who can empathize. Confirm changes by evidence, clients can choose a mantra to help e.g. "1 can do, I will do". Another method is identifying with a person they can aspire to. Stepping into their shoes, seeing, hearing, thinking their mind and explaining what is seen and heard. Clients should keep a journal on their thoughts, feelings and experiences, assisting reflection and encouragement aiding the adjustment of the coaching programme if required.

The tertiary level of coaching

The Tertiary level is concerned with the intense listening skills that are paramount to coaching success. At this level, the focus is on the coachee's "self" awareness or identity through communication, not coachee performance. Promoting self-confidence by acknowledging successes and inwardly promoting self-esteem. Speaking directly to someone is a personal conveyance of expressions of feelings and intent, there is immediate feedback and response to what has been said.

Communication works both ways and positive talkers, an attribute required by the coach and being passed to the coachee, must listen actively in addition to expressing themselves well.

Demonstrated by taking care to verify information is understood by themselves and the coachee.

The most noticeable characteristic of positive talkers is that they project positive expectations, both for themselves and others. The coaching skills is to motivate someone to do what the coach would like them to do, focus on the desirable, positive result, not the negative alternative. Positive talkers' gives credit whenever credit is due, they don't hesitate to applaud others when they succeed. They also give themselves credit whenever they create positive events in their own lives. Positive talkers learn from their experiences and setbacks emerging stronger persons.

The barriers to skilful and powerful communication are both physical and judgmental or view of things. The judgemental or prejudices views, mixed with other ingredients such as not listening properly, misunderstanding, misinterpretation, frustration, loss of essence of what has been said, mentally finishing the sentence and the mind has moved on.

The physical barriers are found mostly found in the working environment because people are not free to converse, offer opinion or vocalize generally. Other issues are; lack of privacy, layout of the room, noise levels, distractions — people comings and goings and boredom of the workplace.

Unfortunately, it is hard to judge if listening, concentrating or interest is being shown. When conversations are relayed, there is the possibility of distortion. All these issues and barriers need to be explored and strategies designed to address these issues.

When the tertiary skills are learnt, the coach and coachee will have a fruitful and successful coaching agreement.

Discuss ending the coaching relationship and outline some key difficulties that coaches and clients may face during this process.

The coach has a professional code of ethics to adhere to, many governed maybe governed by legislative codes in the future.

The coach and client relationship are close and professional, based on understanding the client's open and "hidden" traits, character, personality, views, beliefs, knowledge and skills. When the coaching period ends can be a challenging time for both the coach and the coachee. The coach can feel a sense of pride in the achievements of the client, but a sense of losing a friend, a person that they have nurtured by listening, observing and giving direction. The client can feel lost, the security net will be gone, the sense of the coach not being there to guide and offer support, the person they can trust without question. In the working environment, the client would have the opportunity to seek the advice of the coach if needed.

Although the coaching period would be discussed during the assessment consultation, there can be problems when it ceases, most of the clients will cope well, because of changes in their beliefs, skills learnt, knowledge and flexibility to guide them to achieve their goals with confidence and self — esteem.

The problems are about emotions, the process, first identified by Feud when he observed that clients in therapy began to show unfounded strong feelings for him. The process is known as transference and counter transference. Transference refers to the client to coach transfer and counter transference is vice versa.

Transference is when the client is reminded of experiences from their past, that is said, or done by the coach which is then brought into the present by the client's emotional and psychological needs. This is difficult to recognise, but any extreme emotional responses could be a sign. Transferences can be traumatic and destructive, or love and power depending on the illusions triggered in the client's mind. If the behaviour goes un-noticed or not remedied, the illusions can become an obsession resulting in fantasies, nightmares, poor choices and bad decisions.

To avoid transference difficulties, the coach must not be part of the illusional world of the client. But treat the client and their problems separately, dealing with problems or issues as part of the coaching programme. The coaching programme is based on analysing, planning, working through problems, setting tasks and homework to assist problem solving.

The processes of anchoring and reframing within the context of NLP

Anchors or associations are made between sensations and emotional triggers, if an individual is exposed to a unique stimulus while in an emotional state the connections are made. Anchors can be empowering or disempowering depending on what situation, environment, or thoughts and feelings are brought to the fore in a person's "world", sometimes the anchors will propel the person an emotion without the person being able to cancel it out e.g. a comment made by someone can be the stimulus to trigger a change of mood. The person knows when the anchors are present, and the challenge is recognising that something must be done to overcome these obstacles to success.

Working through a programme, guided by the client's assessment, the coach and client decide on what action is required, considering what triggers negative reactions; what are the sensory modes, gestures, voice tone, facial expressions that change a person's mood. How does the setting or the environment affect the triggers? What and how does these associations link with past experiences and what anchors need to be put into place, either by anchoring by design or anchoring by default.

Reframing, works through changing the way an event is perceived, therefore changing the meaning of that event. When the meaning changes, the consequential responses and behaviour changes. Using effective language with open questions, listening, offering differing view paths will build confidence and rapport to overcome anchors and give the client choice.

The outcome frame must be defined by the client and be achievable, keeping the positive elements of the process. Be compatible and natural with the client's lifestyle, both emotionally and socially. The client must want change to create change, to plan where they are now and what they want to achieve their goals. Construct a plan to show the area of control and influence which will highlight what is required to achieve goals, what can and cannot be done. Looking at skills and experience and available resources amongst colleagues, family and friends.

Our experiences in the past can be re-labelled or re-framed as a valuable lesson or opportunity to grow and extend ourselves. It can endow us with nice qualities of caring and compassion, either way it can determine our future, ultimately the goal is to design a better future.

Describe and discuss the potential of NLP within the coaching programme

Pay specific attention to the following areas and relate them to core concepts within the course material: Outcome Expectation Planning Self-belief

Rehearsal

Achieving goals

Teaching and learning

NLP described as the technology of the mind, the science of achievement and the study of success.' Based upon the search and study of the factors which highlights success or failure in human performance. Identifying the "ingredients" of excellent performance in people, and what people do that is less than expert.

For an individual to reach their goals, expectation of outcome is the first stage of that journey. Wanting change and motivation to take ownership of their goals and understanding the professional and ethical outcomes to achieve those ambitions. Those changes are doing something reasonably well and wanting to do better. Wishing to learn new skills, better communication, adopting improved ways of managing moods, thoughts, other behavioural skills, maybe moving outside the individual's comfort zone.

Benefiting an individual's ambitions and progress, the client's assessment is planned. Using modelling/mapping to overcome negative body language. Anchoring, making associations between sensations and stimulus. Reframing, changing the way an "event" is perceived to change the meaning of that "event". Asking the questions, e.g. "How I deal with unfamiliar situations? And "To what extent do I allow my assumptions of other people expectations of me influence my performance?

Coaching with the client to view motivating factors, what drives the person? External considerations; workplace development/promotion. Personal considerations; health, wealth, relationships, qualifications and popularity. Are the goals realistic? And how will the client know when they or the coach have reached the goals?

Does the client have the self —esteem and confidence to succeed? Beneficial if the coach can empathize with the client to understand the advantages, disadvantages and lost benefits, e.g. loss of popularity or friendships in the workplace. How the client feels after ambitions have been achieved, will the negative behaviours be banished for good.

The coach is the facilitator; dependent on this skill will affect the outcomes for the client. Coaching h communicates the core information or skills that the client may not have, using methods that suits the client's learning style, by notes, verbally explaining or role play. The coach must make sure the client has the resources, tools and people in the workplace to assist the progress. The success of the outcomes is client dependent, the client must utilize every opportunity to mentally plan their goals. Results show that mental rehearsals lead to practical trials; failures not seen as negative but a behaviour changing process. Advising the client to adapt to learning new skills by ridding themselves of limiting beliefs about their capacity to learn. The coach must review the progress being made by the client.

The application of NLP skills follows a format for interview and presentation skills. Requiring expectation of outcomes; research and preparation. Planning; Knowledge of the role, product, company, practiced responses. Presentation; knowledge, visualization, rehearsal, familiarity, and notes. Self-belief; having confidence, rapport, communication skills, being right for the position or having the appropriate interviewing skills. Positive anchoring; visualization of desired outcome, positive projection and appeal. Achieving goals; positive intentions, honesty, spontaneity. An important aspect is learning is relaxing, information is absorbed better, creating a mental map of what must be learnt and reading the information to dramatic effect.

The term "competency skills" in relation to career coaching

and why these skills are relevant to client assessment, particularly regarding the establishment of a collaborative relationship between coach and client.

The term ^Competency skills" is the understanding and knowledge required by the career coach to direct and nurture the client successfully. These skills must be updated on a regular basis to maintain a prominent level of effective and professional competency.

The core inter-linked competency skills are set to professional and ethical standards. This mechanism builds a good, secure working relationship based on acceptance and understanding. They provide collaboration between the coach and client, and the success of the working relationship for the term of the coaching contract.

Empathy, an important core skill provides the basis of the coaching process. To be a good listener, to understand what is being said and why. Listening to summarize, clarify what the client is saying. To understand the client's thoughts, ideas, achievements, disappointments. Questions should be open-ended, allow honesty, allow the client to think.

Genuineness, demonstrated in wanting the client to achieve their goals and aspirations, this encourages the client to be open and honest about their feelings and experiences effectively. Warmth creates an atmosphere of trust, to develop negotiations and mutual respect without crossing the line of professionalism.

Encapsulated in the core quality of warmth are conversational skills, using appropriate language, rate of speech, tone of voice, ensures that positive vibes are expressed; negativity or hostility can affect the client's inability to express their feelings, resulting in a lack of confidence.

Coupled with conversational skills is eye contact, maintaining this reinforces the trust and acceptance between the coach and client. The client gets the undivided attention if there are no distractions.

Facial gestures, the coach should be firm and non-judgemental, but show expressions of affirmation, interest, empathy with smiles, nodding in appropriate places during conversations. Taking note of how and what is being said. Avoidance of protracted debate which can lead to directional leading, clichés and generalizations.

All the competency skills will facilitate the design of the coaching format that will be spontaneous, flexible and open, trusting, energetic, and humorous.

Coachee's values and motivators

Relevant to their present role, and how you would ascertain their skills and interests. In addition, how you would ascertain their wishes regarding skills improvement and enhanced work-related interests

Firstly, I would establish a motivational and collaborative partnership with the coachee to develop their potential. I would ascertain the attitude of the coachee, is the attitudes negative or positive, what factors created the attitude and how I can nurture and maintain a positive attitude. Understand the coachee's ability to absorb knowledge, finding out about their role n — what is enjoyed or not. What interests does the coachee have, what encourages them to do well? What would they like to achieve now and in the future?

Secondly, I would want to know what skills and achievements had been obtained and how those skills could be used to benefit them. Do those achievements need to be expanded on to achieve what they hope to aspire to, is there problem areas e.g. problem solving or communication to resolve? In setting goals, three parts of the body are used. The head, the intellectual side, the hands, the creative side and the heart, the emotional side based on past experiences, a powerful tool in the development of a coachee.

Thirdly, I would build a strategy for the coachee to achieve their goals and ultimately job satisfaction. I would look at the office structure, resources available e.g. training courses, tools available, inspiring environments and contacts that would benefit the coachee's progress. Elements of the process may change but adapting and reviewing those changes the requirements can be met without the loss of enjoyment fulfilling the targets set.

Lastly, to compile a "stepping stones "programme of tasks to gain practical wisdom, knowledge by theory and training by practice. Beginning with the tasks that are easy to complete as way of interest and to set the ground rules to succeeding e.g. concentration, satisfaction, motivation and the enjoyment of the tasks leading to increased anticipation of new knowledge and experience.

The distinct types of interview

and client skill which may need developing, together with how the coaching programme would address these needs.

Think about strategies, types and formats, together with the skills clients will need to address to facilitate a positive outcome.

The phone interview is a popular method with employment agencies, as a form of the initial screening process. Sometimes it is the only form of contact prior to appointment, especially if the position is web based or psychometric tests are involved. The phone interview tests verbal communication, professional manner and conduct. Overall experience is questioned, when candidate is available for appointment, salary expectation, previous employer, education and skills, why wishing to leave current employer. This saves time having initial interviews, but the candidate needs to be prepared for such an interview. This can be done as a homework exercise, and working with the client to rehearse the scenario, using the client's life purpose statement and assessment to coach the techniques required. It has been known that a phone interview can be held as a conference line with several people conversing with the applicant, all this can be rehearsed. This type of interview can be time consuming, the client needs to be well prepared with documents to hand, cv, paper, pen, copy of application form, and ensuing that the environment is peaceful without distraction. Also, importantly remembering that one minute on the phone is like 10 minutes to the mind.

Face-to-face interviews, these are one-to-one meetings between the candidate and the interviewer, popular with many organizations as it brings a personal dimension to the interview. Sometimes there are interviewers from the key areas of the company, making the interview competency based.

Sequential interviews, these are several interviews in turn, with a different interviewer each time representing the different departments within the company. Each interviewer asking questions to test different sets of competencies, these interviewers are skilled in each expected competency. In this situation the candidate will discover that they are answering the same question repeatedly. It is best to keep to the same answer but use different wording to answer equally well. Concentration at the interview is paramount and rehearsing and role play prior to the interview will help greatly.

Panel interviews, involving from two, up to five interviewers, these are usually specialists in their field of work. One person is appointed as chairperson to co-ordinate the smooth conduct of the interview.

Competency based interviews; this type of interview assesses the candidate's ability to perform tasks relevant to the job. The questions are based on scenarios that are likely to take place in the business. The questions are powerful and effective to highlight structured thinking e.g. "if you were faced with how you would handle the situation?" because it brings to the fore the candidate's skill to verbally demonstrate how they would approach, handle and resolve a situation or problem.

Psychometrics interviewing has become popular in corporate companies to assess the candidate's psychological suitability and skills for the job role. The name is given to the study concerned with the theory and technique of educational and psychological measurement. These tests measures personality, attitudes, beliefs and academic achievements. This form of interviewing can be included in competency-based interviews or indeed, be the initial step before a formal interview.

Therefore, interviews can be a combination of diverse types of interview, another example is face to-face interviews can be mixed with a web-based test.

The type and format of an interview is largely based on nature of the company, based on its products, service, culture and management style. Some managers for instance do not like psychometric testing because they feel it reduces the skill of the specialist management team.

Coaches will help the client to prepare for interviews by using the life purpose statements, job criteria based on an action plan of business research. Working on situation scenarios, evaluating the outcomes, building on strengths, weaknesses, skills and abilities. Homework can be for tasks, role play and modelling. Rehearsing possible questions and answers, working on body language, presentation demeanour. Overall the employer is searching in a candidate; teamwork, communication skills, solution-orientated, self-motivation, organizational skills, personality skills, initiative and interpersonal skills.

The most frequent interview questions, and appropriate responses.

Establishing the client's life purpose statement and assessment, using modelling and mapping to identify strengths and weaknesses plus objectives, aims and goals. Assessing financial requirements, knowledge and skills, education, work experience and qualifications. Using role play and rehearsals to test verbal communication and personal presentation skills, the general logistics of being prepared for the interview.

Some corporate companies use psychometric testing, the content is based on set of statements testing academic achievement, knowledge, skills, ability, attitudes, beliefs, psychological profile and other characteristics based on the job analysis.

The questions that are often asked of the candidate are;

"Tell me a little bit about yourself', this question allows a summary of work related qualifications, experience and skill factors.

"What sort of remuneration are you seeking? This question tests negotiating skills, clever idea to check on the internet for the average salary for the chosen field of work if not sure.

"What are your strengths and weaknesses" – the candidate should concentrate on positive skills supported by job related evidence. Weaknesses can be highlighted as "challenges" which have been addressed, overcome and how becoming a strength. These attributes can be discussed during the coaching sessions using modelling and mapping.

"What would be your immediate and long term aims and goals if you were given the position? The candidate can demonstrate how their aims and goals meet with the business requirements. The information regarding the business and the company's mission statement can be sought on the internet.

"Why did you leave/or want to leave?" – The best reply to give is that a more challenging role is sought, current role no longer fulfilling ambitions.

"How soon can you start" — know what the notice period is and holiday commitments.

"What do you want to achieve in 5 years' time?"

State the skills and experience you want to achieve, not the position you want to be in.

If there is more than one interviewer, being a panel interview, the questions are competency based. Sometimes a question is put to the candidate, but in a different format, the candidate should give the same solution, but differently. This type of question can be to test concentration, or the solution is so good that the interviewer wants to hear more on the topic.

Scenario based questions e.g. "if you were forced with ... how you would handle the situation?

This verbally demonstrates how the candidate would approach, handle and resolve the given situation, based on experience or hypothetical solutions. These types of questions are testing the candidate's structured thinking. Using the words "I will, "and "I would" places the candidate in the job role, shows confidence and willingness to work as a team.

The interview skills and strategies are practical, and applications can be rehearsed with the client.

Learning not to respond to a question without thinking, not to look or sound desperate for the job. Homework is the research, planning, rehearsal, responses and letter writing. The coach should assist with the construction of documentation required.

In answering the questions, the candidate should keep in mind the following elements an employer is seeking, with good coaching this should come easy. Initiative, teamwork, communication skills, solution oriented, enthusiasm, energy, self-motivation, goal/result orientated, compatibility, flexibility and organisational skills. Let the employer see your positive and happy face, observe your drive and ambitious face.

IT'S HARD TO TALK ......LIVING WITH DEMENTIA

I am puzzled and perturbed about sense of humour, it was written in a book that having a sense of humour is a gift. But if you have not been blessed with that gift from god then don't try to act as if you have one. This proves good advice, when I hear work colleagues say, "I have forgotten that, I must be going senile". Ha Ha, NOT funny, so why do people do that?

No-one hears anyone joke and laugh about cancer and say, "I don't feel right; I must have cancer". So, why, why do people accept humour about senile dementia.

Does society need educating, maybe so and hopefully during awareness week that fault will be rectified. During awareness week if you get the opportunity to speak with carers, carers who can share their experiences with others.

Watching a person with dementia is a full-time job, 24/7, it's stressful, tormenting and heart breaking beyond words. Watching your father or mother forgetting who you are, at times recognising you, but sadly forgetting your name. going back in time and you become their brother or sister. Explaining the facts and details only creates anguish and internal suffering; you can feel their organs tremble. Tears are shed by the bucketful for loss is seen bit by bit, until the day arrives when you watch the person sleeping day by day and I won't tell you the cruel ending. Faith is tested to the core, and we know it's strong.

So be gentle, be kind, don't argue or fight back, the fear and anguish in the middle of the night for a job they are anxious to do, assuring them that the task was done, and all is calm again.

Keep them safe as if a new-born child, welcome to the world of dementia

Thankfully, due to the work of organisations and individuals, society has become aware of the needs of those suffering with this dreadful illness.

Anna

THE VALUE OF A SMILE

"It cost nothing but creates much, it enriches those who receive without

Impoverishing those who give"

Over the years I heard stories from people who have lived in the same area since childhood.

I remember an elderly lady relating the times as a young mother, she travelled to the forest for picnics with her children. Meeting up with other families, revelling in the wide-open space of the countryside with its river and meadow flowers .... A real treat in those days.

The story from a much-loved member of the parish of how, ladies of the parish would collect old woollen garments, undo them and sell the balls of wool to raise funds to build the church.

Working together to build important things, let's ensure that this philosophy survives the passage of time.

Anna

Angela's journey through career coaching

Career Coaching is very rewarding, maintaining the ethics, legal compliance and the code of conduct required to nurture and identify Angela's life purpose, supporting them towards their aims and goals. Showing empathy, genuineness, communication, trust, being energetic in outlook, all the core coaching skills required. Discovering the factors that hinder the achievements of those aspirations and trying to overcome those obstacles.

Using the building block method to view personality, character traits, skills, influences, achievements, interests, problem areas and motivators. Viewing negative factors, how they occurred and how to turn that energy into positive vibes.

The client assessment, coupled with good rapport, builds confidence, mutual trust and respect. The financial aspects and confidentiality agreement agreed and signed, the client assessment was then studied in detail.

Angela's requirements were assessed, getting to know her personality and character traits. The qualities she has to offer, setting goals, getting accepted in the organization. Selling her, achieving status and excellence. The human being has three centres of learning, the head, the heart and the hands. The balance is getting these factors right. If we are not happy then, the right balance has not been achieved.

Angela is positive with an extrovert personality, but lacks confidence in her own abilities, this lack of confidence causes her to pay too much attention to other people's perception leading to lower confidence, and a covert tendency then hides a lot of her talents. Angela is a competent Senior Credit Controller but wants to extend her knowledge to another area of the organization. Angela's strengths are; effective communication, numerical skills, motivation and achievement of business targets. Other skills; good planning collating information, analysing, predicting, assessing and interpreting information and encouraging others. I used direct coaching encouraging her to make decisions, perceiving the future without the problems. Also, Secondary level coaching to uncover the contributing factors in her subconscious that influences the lack of confidence. Next step was visualising her role model, which is modelling/mapping, mirroring the person she aspires to be like. Anchoring, important to assess the bad emotions involved and reframing flaws into becoming positive attributes. The outcome hierarchy to practice behaviours and thoughts to promote confidence, to take ownership of the situation. Expectation of outcome, Angela must want change; a good homework exercise is visualization, whereby she places herself in the chosen role, hearing herself speak. Encouraging confidence, self —belief and motivation. Also promoting self-confidence by acknowledging successes and inwardly promoting self-esteem and learning to relax. Another aid is research and preparation about her new role in the business. Angela's will have an overall view of herself for the new role and a positive future.

Angela wants to develop as a specialist in the customer care division of her organization. Discussing her core skills and how these suits the new role. Angela wants to expand her expertise of the business to reach her goal of being part of the training team. It was useful using Maslow's pyramid to set the route to the top goal. Deciding the support required from peers and mentors, Time, resources, access to training tools and understanding management priorities in the new role

The CV/curriculum vitae presented professionally eye catching but not artistic, concise English on one sheet of A4 paper. Using bullet points for each experience, showing the suitability for the position applied for, strengths and weaknesses, highlighting how these are being overcome.

Choosing an appropriate template, demonstrating Angela's ability to communicate, reliable, a team player, competent and other positive characteristics and skills. Crucial information must be accurate, employment dates, job titles and roles defined, any gaps being accounted for.

Qualifications listed correctly, interests declared. Angela will be using her current skill set in her new position, therefore one CV will be appropriate, if Angela digresses into another work sphere, then a differing CV would be submitted. Current Referees and highlighted good references. The CV was accurately addressed with a covering letter. Angela completed a general Job Search Evaluation; the suggestions can be adapted to suit Angela's future aims.

Angela, who wishes to stay within the organisation, must create a marketing strategy for her image, talents and skills. Working together, we created a marketing plan, which will always be useful.

VISUALIZATION TECHNIQUES

FIND A QUIET PLACE

Define your objective/goal/aim

Concentrate on the breath and breathing; slow. Breathing through the nose and out through the mouth.

Begin your visualization by using a chosen image, a scene, a person... something or someone special helps to recall the image whenever visualization is undertaken.

Once the image has been placed in the mind, now place yourself in that image too.

Hear yourself speak to the person in your scene, see yourself in the role that you want to be in.

this visualization technique can be done at any time and several times to encourage confidence, self -belief and motivation.

A very useful tool when faced with speaking to an audience or facing a daunting meeting with the boss.

Enjoy the experience and Good Luck

"I am fed up, I want to be anywhere but here "

How many times a week do we hear those words in the workplace, several times I guess.

After all, we are controlled by emotions and feelings, that in turn govern our thoughts for the good or bad.

Negative emotions, thoughts and feelings also lowers our immune system, depresses our mental function and capability.

Thus, inhibiting physical accomplishment of achieving our aims and goals.

Positive emotions have the opposite effect and boosts the immune system causing the brain to work in a balanced mode which is conductive to change.

NEVER TRY TO FORCE POSITIVITY IT CREATES AN IMBALANCE …. Pretending to be happy, when clearly you are not.

The act of forcing control of any situation can impede flexibility and create rigid goals which are unachievable, because there is a weak link between body and mind.

That's why we all need to know yourselves, what makes us happy and contented, what makes us achieve our aims.

Setting expectations too high or concentrating exclusively on goals can have a negative outcome.

Being too mindful of what other people think or taking opinions to heart too can readily lead to non-acceptance of self and therefore compromise identity.

If an individual has a closed mind to change or other people's opinions or facts, limits choices and impairs achievements of goals. This frame of mind often presents as unfounded anger, overt independence and refusing the help or the company of others associated with the same tasks.

So, concentrate on the present and plan.,

Role Model at Play

This method learning is favoured by many career coaches and training departments. Some staff enjoy the chance to be an acting star for a short while, others dread the moment the spotlight is on them.

This new role play is more personal and easy to be controlled by the individual.

Clients are encouraged to identify someone that they aspire to or who has already made the changes that they desire too. So, it can be famous or someone nearer to home.

The key element is that they must be the total embodiment of the client's desired changes.

This is how it works;

1. Imagine that the person is standing in front of him/her.

2. Imagine they are surrounded by an invisible shell

3. Unzip the shell and step in

4. Now see, hear and think through their mind.

Explain what they see and hear.

Proves an Interesting insight into the individuals

Lack of Listening and Concentrating

Pre-judging someone's listening ability because of age or circumstance is a barrier to effective communication

If the working environment and expectations of those in senior positions identifies lack of skills or experience, or indeed lack of confidence, then a listening barrier may occur because the individual will be focusing on their perceived shortcomings rather than what is being asked of them.

We all need to be motivated to listen, boredom together with an uninteresting environment can create a barrier to effective listening.

Some individuals have difficulty concentrating for lengthy periods of time, a barrier to listening effectively. Some people find note taking helps to keep the mind focused.

The following physical barriers to listening are sometimes ignored, these are;

Lack of privacy

The way the desks are arranged

Noise levels

Distractions

People traffic; the comings and goings.

Lack of verbal communication

Within the working environment people are not as free to converse, offer opinion, or vocalize generally, as they would within a social environment. Therefore, a strong need to think and plan speech before it is uttered.

Individuals need to think about what they wish to say, how best to convey it. It is much easier to adopt the jargon of the workplace – we all do this, and it helps to feel included to feel included and gives self-confidence.

Simple language is the best way to communicate, in other words, clear and concise.

Hot Tips;

Be economical with words, so use as few words as possible to get the point across

Pronounce technical or unusual words clearly and be prepared to repeat or clarify them

Unless presenting from another medium it is best that individuals speak in their own words so that they convey sincerity and confidence; this helps nervousness

Speaking directly to someone allows for expression of feelings and intent. The individuals will get immediate feedback and response to what has been said.

Unfortunately, it can often be hard to judge if someone is listening, concentrating or interested in what is being said. It is not a permanent record unless the conversion is recorded in some formal way. When conversation is relayed, embellishment or distortions may be included. There is also a risk of clashes or loss of temper when conversations turn into heated debates or arguments.

All these issues need to be explored and strategies thought about.

From the little room

On the 4th May 2015 I had the opportunity to attend the book launch of the book entitled "In Pursuit of Success", the story of Leader, an advertising company, celebrating its 50th anniversary.

At the heart of the business was the leader, Bryan Holden. The business was brought to life and it grew and continues to thrive under the leadership of the next generation of his family.

Their business philosophy, they have a series of values, courage, and a belief in their team of staff. They have a belief in delivering the WOW factor and having a passion for what they do.

The business has always been keen to develop the staff, unlocking peoples talents or "gifts" as they like to call them by investing in the training and development.

Their business ethics;

Your company is a living, breathing entity, keep it well nourished

Your employees are all important, they are the company's most asset.

Always think positive, negative thoughts only breed negativity.

BUSINESS

FOR

EVERYBODY

This something I heard a few years ago, where it came from, I don't know

This is the story of four people named *Everybody, Somebody, Anybody and Nobody.* There was an important job to be done and *Everybody* was asked to do it.

Anybody could have done it, but *Nobody* did it.

Somebody got angry about that, because it was *Everybody's* job.

Everybody thought Anybody *could do it,* but *Nobody* realized that *Everybody* wouldn't do it.

Consequently, it wound up that *Nobody* told *Anybody, so Everybody blamed Somebody*

The Famous Two

In 1935, Alfred McAlpine, fourth son of Sir Robert McAlpine, the founder of the family construction empire, chose to break away from the main family company and remain with his son and a few loyal colleagues in the north-west.

The company grew from strength, from early contracts, grim locations, long hours, the recession and then the war. The company provided underground storage, shadow factories, aerodromes, power stations and opencast mining to fuel the nation's needs.

After the war, the company was a substantial force in the civil engineering circle and the work flooded in. rebuilding factories and the infrastructure, preparing rocket sites for defence., Britain was rising from the debris after the war.

What stood out was the spirit of the company, the men who worked together to make the company a household name. Their loyalty, their sense of humour and the asset of working hard.

The company had exciting times, tough times and challenging times both at home and overseas.

To this day, Sir Alfred McAlpine Civil Construction Company is still talked about with pride and affection. Why? Because the company in turn respected their employees.

The Power of Communication at Its Best

This is a fabulous story to tell, it highlights the ability of colleagues working together to succeed in a project. It highlights how Senior Management respected their staff and knew that they could succeed at what they were asked to do.

In the early seventies a large steel contract was taking place in Scunthorpe, it was one of the biggest projects of its kind since the war.

It was remarkable on two counts; the size and value of the contract and it was the one large project undertaken by Sir Alfred McAlpine and Sir Robert McAlpine firms jointly.

The bringing together of the two companied caused apprehension amongst the workers in both camps. I guess, it was probably the old thought of "the them and us "syndrome. Coupled with the fact that both companies were developed along different lines.

Sir Alfred McAlpine was controlled from the Wolverhampton office And Sir Robert McAlpine controlled from the south. The overall project manager was Alan Darton from Sir Robert's McAlpine did a magnificent job.

And this is where professionalism at its very best comes into play.

Alan Darton decided from the start that he was going to have one cohesive team, and that he was not going to tolerate any nonsense in the form of rivalry between the men of the two companies.

In this way he created a completely close-knit and compatible team from the two staffs.

The job went exceptionally well, completed on time.

And both companies' directors were delighted

It was a very real example of how two very different companies could be welded into a successful team, provided that the will was there on the part of the man directing the project.

As well as exemplary relations with their clients, both in the private and public sectors. Sir Alfred McAlpine always enjoyed a unique relationship with their staff and with the workforce under their control.

As someone said to Sir Bobby McAlpine

"Your Group has a chemistry which many others would like to have"

How many companies can claim that statement today!

A SUCCESSFUL COMPANY/BUSINESS RECOGNISES;

Talent

Skills

Development

Communication

LEADS TO;

Respect

Loyalty

LEADS TO;

Achievements

Profit

Customer Satisfaction

Good Luck

And

Best Wishes

For

The future